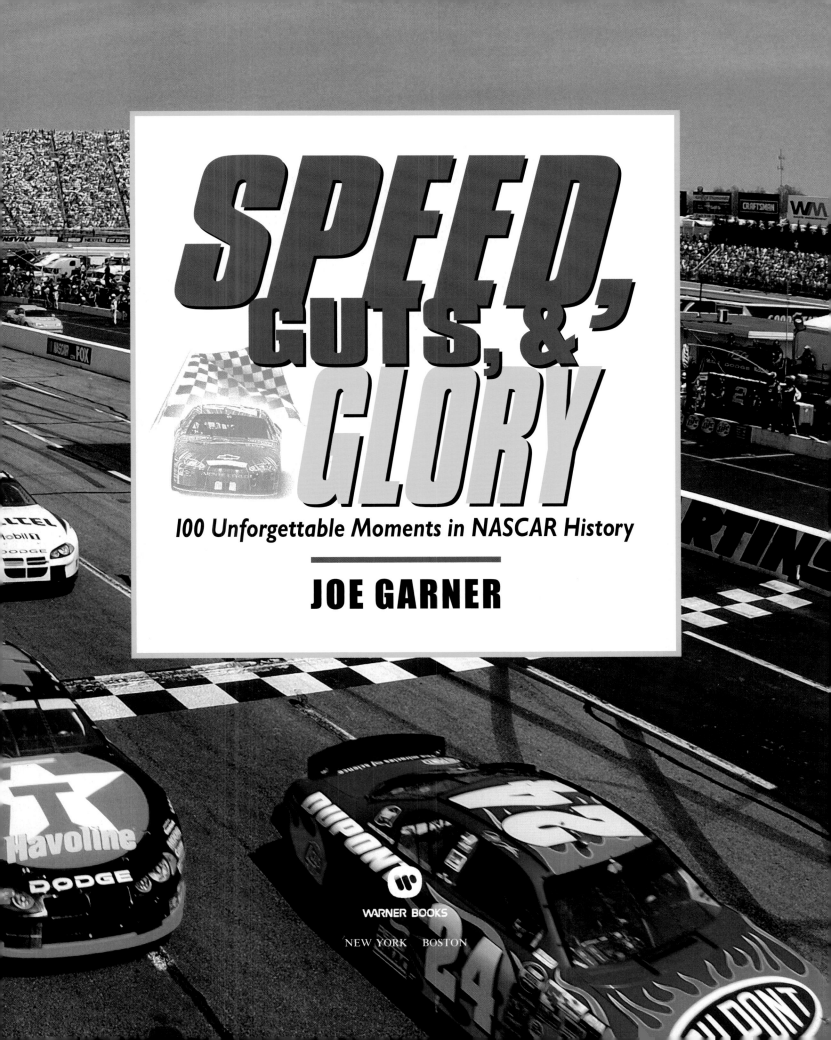

SPEED, GUTS, & GLORY

100 Unforgettable Moments in NASCAR History

JOE GARNER

WARNER BOOKS

NEW YORK   BOSTON

• • •

BOOK CREDITS

Editorial and text assistance provided by Lynnsey Guerrero, Stuart Miller, Todd Schindler, Bill Stroum
Story consultant, Don Smyle; Photo editor, Abigail Ray

• • •

DVD CREDITS

Executive producer, Joe Garner
Host, Jeff Gordon
Narration, Ryan McGee; Project director, Gerry Martin
Director of photography, Al Francesco; Producer, Joe Ligon
Camera operator, Gary Johnson; Teleprompter operator, Bill Barnes
Audio technician, Chris Horton; Makeup artist, Rebecca Jones; Lighting director, Frank Freas
Studio production facilities provided by MediaComm, Charlotte, NC
Postproduction provided by NASCAR Images, Charlotte, NC
Footage is courtesy of NASCAR Images
`NASCAR Digital Entertainment, LLC. All rights reserved.

• • •

WARNER BOOKS
Printed in the United States of America

First Edition: November 2006
10 9 8 7 6 5 4 3 2 1

• • •

Library of Congress Cataloging-in-Publication Data

Garner, Joe.
Speed, guts, and glory : 100 unforgettable moments in NASCAR history / Joe Garner. — 1st ed.
p. cm.
Summary: "Captures the exciting finishes, the terrifying crashes, and the heartbreaking
tragedies of the uniquely American popular sport of stockcar racing." —Provided by the publisher.
ISBN–13: 978-0-446-57988-9
ISBN–10: 0-446-57988-2
1. Stock car racing—United States—History. 2. NASCAR (Association)—History. I. Title.
GV1029.9.S74G37 2006
796.720973—dc22   2006011604

• • •

Book Design: Judith Turziano

• • •

PHOTOGRAPHY CREDITS

© *Alan Schein Photography/CORBIS:* XII; *AP Photo:* XVI–1, 10–11, 16–17, 20–21, 29, 31, 36–37, 44–45,
51, 52–53, 55, 63, 71, 72–73, 75, 76–77, 78, 80–81, 83, 86, 89, 92–93, 100, 150–151, 152–153, 162,
166–167, 176–177, 182, 187, 208–209, 220, 222–223, 230–231, 239; *Bill Hall/Getty Images:* 181;
Brian Cleary/Getty Images: 124; *Cameras in Action Stock Photography, Inc.:* 184, 189; *Chris Stanford/Getty Images:* 2, 4,
134, 236–237; *Darrell Ingham/Getty Images:* 126, 130, 219; *David Taylor/Getty Images:* 99; *Donald Miralle/Getty Images:* 141;
Dozier Mobley: 18, 28, 34, 47, 54, 59, 62, 94–95, 102, 103, 105, 108–109, 115, 118–119, 148, 164, 165, 174 (both),
179, 190, 202, 206, 226, 234–235; *Focus on Sport/Getty Images:* 110, 138–139, 161; *Frances Flock:* 218, 233;
© *George Tiedemann/NewSport/Corbis:* II–III, 120–121; *Getty Images:* 168–169; *Icon SMI/Corbis:* 216–217;
Jamie Squire/Getty Images: 3, 22; *Jim Gund/Getty Images:* 156–157; *Jonathan Ferrey/Getty Images:* 6–7, 56–57, 112–113, 132–133;
Julian Gonzales/Getty Images: 186–187; © *Larry Kasperek/New Sport/Corbis:* 48–49; *Motorsports Images and Archives Photography:* 8–9, 12,
13–14, 26(left), 26–27, 38, 40–41, 42, 50, 60–61, 84–85, 90–91, 106–107, 125, 127, 129, 136, 142–143, 146–147(all), 158–159,
170–171, 172–173, 200–201, 204, 210, 214–215; *Pal Parker Archives:* 65, 66–67, 68–69, 154, 192–193, 194, 195, 197, 198,
212–213, 225, 228; *Ray Shough and Bristol Motor Speedway:* 79(all); *Robert Laberge/Getty Images:* 32–33, 116, 229;
© *Sam Sharpe/Corbis:* XI, 24–25; © *Sutton Motorsport Images/Corbis:* 144–145, 221; *Vincent Laforet/Getty Images:* 96–97, 122–123;
© *William R. Sallaz/NewSport/Corbis:* XIII; *WINN ©Reuters/CORBIS:* XIV
Illustrations by *John Corbitt/Duet Studio*

For Colleen,
J.B., and Jillian…
and the fans.

CONTENTS

Watch this moment with NASCAR Cup champion Jeff Gordon.

ACKNOWLEDGMENTS • X / INTRODUCTION • XII

• • • *Chapter One* • • •

CHASE TO THE CHECKERED FLAG: THE CLOSEST FINISHES

Busch and Craven's 2003 Darlington Duel   2

2001 Atlanta: "This One's for Dale"   5

1993 Talladega: Earnhardt and Irvan   9

1959 Daytona 500: The First Photo Finish   10

1984 Talladega: Cale Yarborough Barely Captures Eightieth Victory   12

1991 Michigan: Jarrett and Allison in a Ford Shootout   13

2004 Texas: Sadler and Kahne's Wheel-to-Wheel Finish   15

1992 Points Race: Kulwicki Takes the Cup on Fumes   18

1992 Winston: Davey Allison Spins Across the Finish Line   19

2005 Atlanta: Carl Edwards Flips for His Wins   23

• • • *Chapter Two* • • •

CINDERELLA MEN: THE UNLIKELIEST VICTORIES

Derrike Cope's 1990 Daytona Surprise   26

Kyle Petty: The First Third-Generation Cup Victory   30

Bobby Labonte Snatches the Last Winston Cup   33

Mark Martin's Lap Lapse at Bristol 1994   34

Jeremy Mayfield Ends His Four-Year Winless Streak   35

The Little Black Taxi That Could   37

NASCAR's Newly Minted "Million-Dollar Bill"   39

Tiny's Big Win at 1963 Daytona 500   42

Jeff Gordon's Bittersweet Win at Martinsville 2005   43

Reversal of Fortune: The 1989 All-Star Challenge at Charlotte   46

AVID PEAR

• • • *Chapter Three* • • •
THE DOMINATORS

Richard Petty: Long Live the King (Richard Petty's Crowning Victory)   **50**
Dale Earnhardt: The Man in Black   **55**
Jeff Gordon: The First of NASCAR's New Breed   **56**
David Pearson: The Silver Fox   **58**
Cale Yarborough: The Timmonsville Flash   **60**
Darrell Waltrip: A Force to Be Reckoned With   **62**
Rusty Wallace: One of the All-Time Greats   **63**
Ned Jarrett: Gentleman Ned   **64**
Bobby Allison: Raging Rebel   **66**
Tim Flock: The Highest-Flying Flock   **70**

• • • *Chapter Four* • • •
"THEY ACTUALLY WALKED AWAY?!"

2005 Talladega: The Biggest Big One   **74**
1990 Bristol: Mikey's Miracle   **79**
Talladega 2003: Sadler's Flip-Flopping Ford   **80**
Talladega 1998: Labonte Escapes a Big One to Take the Checkered Flag   **82**
Talladega 1993: Rusty Wallace's Flying Finish   **84**
Daytona 1988: The King's Worst Crash   **86**
Talladega 1987: Bobby Allison Flies Toward the Grandstands   **87**
Daytona 1984: Ricky Rudd's Crash at the Clash   **88**
Bristol 2002: Harmon's Close Call   **91**
Darlington 1965: Cale's Moon Shot   **94**

• • • *Chapter Five* • • •
THE RECORD BREAKERS

Jeff Gordon's Season to Remember   **98**
Handsome Harry's Amazing Streak   **101**
Bobby Isaac's Twenty Poles in '69   **103**
Bill Elliott: NASCAR's Fastest Driver   **104**
Richard Petty: The Babe Ruth of NASCAR   **106**
Andretti/Foyt: Daytona and Indy Champions   **108**
Dale Jr. Tames Talladega   **111**
David Pearson at the Pole   **114**
Busch the Younger Is the Youngest   **117**
Waltrip's Modern-Era Mark   **117**

• • • *Chapter Six* • • •
THE BEST ROOKIES OF THE YEAR

Tony Stewart, 1999   **122**
Matt Kenseth, 2000   **127**
Ron Bouchard, 1981   **128**
Jamie McMurray, 2003   **130**
Kevin Harvick, 2001   **131**
Ryan Newman, 2002   **132**
Davey Allison, 1987   **135**
Jeff Gordon, 1993   **137**
Kasey Kahne, 2004   **140**
Dale Earnhardt, 1980   **142**

• • • *Chapter Seven* • • •
THE DAYTONA 500: THE GREAT AMERICAN RACE

Petty and Pearson: Legends Collide at the 1976 Daytona 500   **146**
1979 Daytona 500: The Rumble in the Infield   **150**
2001 Daytona 500: A Legend Is Lost   **152**
1988 Daytona 500: Allison versus Allison   **155**
1993 Daytona 500: "Come on Dale, Go Baby Go!"   **156**
1981 Daytona 500: A Win Fit for a King   **158**
1989 Daytona 500: Waltrip's Lucky 17   **160**
2002 Daytona 500: Marlin Bends the Rules   **163**
Janet Guthrie: The First Woman of the Great American Race   **164**
2004 Daytona 500: Junior Wins!   **166**

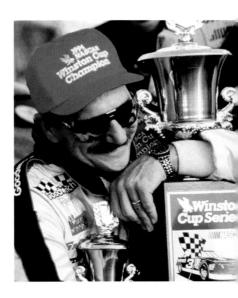

• • • *Chapter Eight* • • •
DALE EARNHARDT: THE INTIMIDATOR

Daytona 500 Victory: Twenty Years in the Making   171
Dale Rides the Air at Talladega   175
"The Intimidator" Is Born   178
Earnhardt Ties the King in Cup Titles   180
The Intimidator Returns   183
The Dogfight at Bristol   184
Earnhardt and Gordon Battle at the Brickyard   185
From Rookie of the Year to Cup Champion   187
The Man in Black/The Man of Steel   188
A First for the Number 3   191

• • • *Chapter Nine* • • •
ONE-WIN WONDERS

Wendell Scott: The First African American Driver to Win at NASCAR's Top Level   194
Richard Brickhouse's Day in the Talladega Sun   198
Ron Bouchard: A New England Yankee in a Southerners' Sport   199
Mark Donohue: Captain Nice   202
Shorty Rollins: NASCAR's First Ever Rookie of the Year   203
Phil Parsons: Victim of the Talladega Curse   205
Lake Speed: A Banner Day at Darlington   207
Buddy Shuman: A Legend in His Own Time   210
Jim Hurtubise: Racing's Lazarus   211
Frankie Schneider: The Old Master at Old Dominion   213

• • • *Chapter Ten* • • •
NASCAR'S DYNASTIES

The France Family: NASCAR's First Family   219
The Pettys: NASCAR's Royal Family   222
The Allisons: NASCAR's "Alabama Gang"   224
The Woods: NASCAR's Oldest Team   227
Hendrick: The Empire That Rick Built   229
The Jarretts: A Championship Family   230
The Flocks: NASCAR's Wild Bunch   232
Richard Childress: NASCAR's Most Intimidating Team Owner   234
Jack Roush: NASCAR Team Titan   237
Junior Johnson: Notorious Bootlegger to NASCAR Icon   238

ACKNOWLEDGMENTS

Just like any winning driver, I am beholden to the support of a dedicated team.

My sincerest gratitude to Jamie Raab and Warner Books for giving me this opportunity. I feel fortunate to be with such a dynamic publisher. And to my editor, Colin Fox, for his invaluable guidance and enthusiasm.

As always, thank you to my agent, Sloan Harris, for his wise and savvy counsel and most of all his friendship.

I am profoundly grateful to Jeff Gordon for contributing his talent, expertise, and integrity to this project. It's an honor working with him.

A very special thank-you to John Bickford of Jeff Gordon, Inc. for seeing the potential in this project from the beginning. It's little wonder that Jeff is so successful after spending time with John.

Thank you to Jeannette Eaves at Jeff Gordon, Inc., for presenting my proposal to John, and for her graciousness and skillful coordination.

I am grateful to Abigail Ray, whom I cannot thank enough. She is enormously talented and able to wear many hats...most times simultaneously. And as I've noted in the past, she does it all with grace, enthusiasm, and a wonderful sense of humor.

A special thank-you to Lynnsey Guerrero for his boundless enthusiasm, creativity, talent, and knowledge of all things NASCAR.

I am grateful to NASCAR Images for joining me in this venture; in particular, Jay Abraham and Jill MacPhee for their determination to "make it work." Thank you to Gary Ramsey for his skill and patience in hammering out our agreement. Thank you to Gerry Martin for his creativity, enthusiasm, and skillful coordination of our production. I am grateful to Don Smyle for enthusiastically sharing his invaluable expertise on NASCAR's history. And thank you to Ryan McGee for his crisp and entertaining narration. A big thank-you to Joe Ligon for a masterful job in producing the DVD segments.

Thank you to Frank and Mable Scott for sharing their personal history in order that we may have a better perspective on the legacy of Wendell Scott.

As always, thank you to my friends Louise Argianas and Wendy Heller-Stein for their support.

Special thank-yous to two integral members of the GCC "pit crew": Janel Syverud, for always making sure there's gas in the tank; and to Scott Sturgis for making sure that information flows.

Thank you to the following people for their determination in providing us with the very best images: Regalle Asuncion and Heidi Schaffner at AP Images; Alexis Kerr at Motorsports Images & Archives; Jennifer Rose and Jason Sundberg at Getty Images; Dozier Mobley, Pal Parker, and Francis Flock.

I am always grateful to Bill Kurtis and Bob Costas for being there in the beginning.

And finally, my deepest gratitude to my wife Colleen, my son James (J.B.), and my daughter Jillian. This is only possible because of their love and unwavering devotion. I am grateful to my parents, Jim and Betty Garner, for their love and for instilling in me the belief that anything is possible; and to Jerry and Sandi Barnes for their continuing love and encouragement.

INTRODUCTION

Ever since my first book, *We Interrupt This Broadcast*, in 1998, I have been exploring the historical pop-culture landscape of America. In that book, and in the eight that have followed, I have chronicled the nation's landmark events in broadcast news, sports, television, famous films, and comedy, employing a multimedia approach that brings together text and photographs with archival audio, video, and film. It has been gratifying that these books have done well on the shelves, but more gratifying still to hear from hundreds of readers, teachers, and librarians who have told me that my work has managed to "bring history to life." I'm lucky enough to have been able to turn a genuine passion into a career and to share that passion with others.

So why NASCAR?

The story of NASCAR racing is little more than six decades old. It's a homegrown American sport that had its modest beginnings, just after World War II, in the rural Southeast, where bootleggers and farmers dueled each other in souped-up jalopies on dirt tracks for nothing but bragging rights and pocket money. Today, those backwoods tracks have become mammoth superspeed-ways, the rambling wrecks have given way to technologically advanced, custom-built monster machines, and daredevil drivers now risk their lives at speeds of more than 200 mph in pursuit of billions in sponsorship, merchandising, and prize money. By any measure, NASCAR's growth has been phenomenal.

Yet the sport remains steeped in the traditions, values, and ideals of its origins. Among the hundreds of thousands that pack the grandstands on race week-ends are scores of families, sometimes two and three generations' worth, for whom racing is as much a tradition as church on Sunday. Ask yourself, what other professional sport begins each event with a prayer before the national anthem? NASCAR is a major cultural phenomenon no matter how you cut it.

There is nothing quite like the experience of a NASCAR race. It's a total assault on the senses. If you're lucky enough to have attended one, you know exactly what I'm talking about. If you haven't, there's really no way to adequately describe it. As my friend and long-time NASCAR enthusiast Lynnsey Guerrero pointed out, it's difficult to make the experience sound the least bit enjoyable. The crowds are enormous. Parking is impossible. You have to get to the track long before the race begins or you run the risk of miss-ing the start altogether. If you don't leave before the checkered flag falls, you'll be stuck in traffic for hours. And of course, it's chest-rattlingly, earsplittingly loud! But no first-timer leaves the track unchanged. Once you've been baptized in sweat and the smell of gasoline and the thunder of forty-three 800-horsepower engines, you're a fan for life.

And simply put, there's no fan like a NASCAR fan. Unique in professional sports is the almost familial bond between NASCAR's stars and the folks in the stands. To the fans, these drivers are bona fide American heroes, but they aren't a breed apart; often they seem as familiar as a brother, an uncle, or a neighbor down the street. Why? Because they're *approachable*. From the moment they step out of their luxury motor homes until they climb into their cars, NASCAR drivers are mingling with the crowd, shaking hands and chatting with well-wishers, posing for

pictures, signing autographs. There are no crowd barriers to scale, no security details to breach. Every fan can rub elbows with the greats. Imagine standing at the free-throw line at the Staples Center before a big game, walking up to Kobe Bryant, and saying, "Hey, Kobe, when you're done shooting, would you mind signing my ball?" It would never happen. But it happens all the time in NASCAR. And the fans repay the favor in unswerving loyalty—to their favorite drivers and to the sport as a whole. Such unfettered access is a huge part of NASCAR's success, and everyone associated with the sport knows it, accepts it, and embraces it.

So, "why NASCAR?" Because the sport is now woven into our pop culture. With its rich history and colorful characters, its grand traditions and thrilling moments, NASCAR has become part of our national mythology. And if you are among the NASCAR faithful who regularly attend the races or those who are grateful for the television coverage, this book is for you.

From the moment I began working on *Speed, Guts, and Glory*, you, the fans, were foremost in my mind. I wanted to create a book that put you trackside to relive some of the greatest moments in NASCAR history. I wanted to make it fun to read and to illustrate it with compelling and dramatic photographs. I also wanted you to be able to experience the sights, sounds, and thrills of NASCAR by including race footage on the DVD. Not only will you read about Richard Petty and David Pearson colliding at the 1976 Daytona 500, the razor-thin door-to-door finish of Kurt Busch and Ricky Craven at Darlington in 2003, and the biggest of the bone-jarring "Big Ones" at Talladega in 2005, you'll also be able to watch them, along with many other high-speed, fender-bending, metal-swapping, second-splitting thrills from NASCAR's glorious history.

Selecting the moments to include in *Speed, Guts, and Glory* wasn't easy. There are 100 stories here, the most I have ever included in any of my books. I chose them based on what I believe fans hope for in a race: exciting door-to-door finishes; unexpected come-from-behind victories; daring performances by racing's dominant drivers; and crashes, as long as everybody walks away. NASCAR and many stock car racing publications have compiled lists season after season of what they consider to be the most significant moments of each year. After culling through those lists, aided by the expert opinions of NASCAR archivist Don Smyle, writer Ryan McGee, and others, I settled on these stories. I hope you'll find some of your favorites among them. I also decided to include tribute sections dedicated to the pioneers of the sport, the Daytona 500, and Dale Earnhardt.

NASCAR Images was also instrumental in helping me select the best broadcast footage for the featured story of each chapter on the DVD.

As important as finding the right material was choosing the right host to present the ten moments highlighted on the DVD. I am thrilled that four-time NASCAR Cup champion and driver of the number 24 DuPont Chevy, Jeff Gordon, accepted my invitation. What impressed me from the start about Jeff was his genuine interest in the history of the sport. His amazing accomplishments, coupled with his knowledge, talent, and warm personality, made him the perfect choice to host the DVD. It has been an honor and a pleasure working with Jeff, his stepfather John Bickford, Jeanette Eaves, and everyone at Jeff Gordon Incorporated.

I hope this book and DVD provide you with hours of entertainment as you relive six full decades of NASCAR's legends and legendary moments—a remarkable history of speed, guts, and glory.

Enjoy the ride.

Chapter One

CHASE TO THE CHECKERED FLAG

The Closest Finishes

Neither driver backed off,
neither driver flinched.
And for the first time in a long while,
a race was decided by a driver's nerve,
not an over-engineered car.

Busch and Craven's 2003 Darlington Duel

• • • • • • • • • •

Ricky Craven doesn't look much like a race car driver, doesn't talk like one—probably a result of growing up in Newburgh, Maine. He has the credentials, though; you don't land a Nextel Cup ride without winning at every level. But in a sport that prides itself

(Overleaf): This image retrieved from the NASCAR scoring camera positioned at the start/finish line shows how Ricky Craven (32) beats Kurt Busch by .002 seconds to win the Carolina Dodge Dealers 400 at Darlington Raceway, Sunday, March 16, 2003 in Darlington, S.C.

(Below): Ricky Craven speeds around the track in the #32 Pontiac.

on fan accessibility to its stars, it's easy to see how someone who comes off rather quiet and unassuming can get buried in the residual glow from current favorites like Dale Jr., Jeff Gordon, and Tony Stewart.

But there was a moment on the afternoon of March 16, 2003—a very, *very* brief moment—that changed everything for Ricky Craven.

Officially, the length of time it took to catapult Craven from a someone-else-in-the-field to someone in the NASCAR record book was 0.002 seconds, about how long it takes for a light bulb to glow after you flip the switch. Snap your fingers or blink your eyes; each action lasts about two thousandths of a second.

That magic number—0.002—is the margin of Ricky Craven's victory over Kurt Busch in what was and most likely will always be remembered as the

Craven passes Kurt Busch, driver of the #97 Rubbermaid Ford, on the final lap before becoming the eventual winner of the NASCAR Carolina Dodge Dealers 400.

most exciting finish in NASCAR racing.

It was that close, that exciting, and that amazing.

The fifth race of the season found the drivers in Darlington for the Carolina Dodge Dealers 400. The historic 1.366-mile, egg-shaped oval was NASCAR's first superspeedway, and since the inaugural 1950 race it has been considered one of the most treacherous tracks in the sport. With mismatched turns at either end, each with a different degree of banking, plus a

concrete retaining wall that seems inexplicably to inch just far enough out to carve a jagged abrasion along the right side of a race car, pretty much from front fender to rear quarter panel, known with exasperated affection as the "Darlington Stripe," it has truly earned its nickname: The Track Too Tough to Tame.

The weekend didn't begin well for Kurt Busch, the twenty-four-year-old driver feeling his way into a third Winston Cup season. He was forced to start in the last row after changing engines following Saturday practice. Busch was also racing on parts and pieces borrowed from his Roush Racing teammates. "I had Mark Martin's springs, Jeff Burton's sway bar, and Matt Kenseth's shocks." But the combination clicked; after the green flag fell the number 97 Rubbermaid Ford was able to juke its way forward through the slower traffic.

Dale Earnhardt Jr. and Mark Martin dominated, combining to lead 162 of the 293 laps, but their

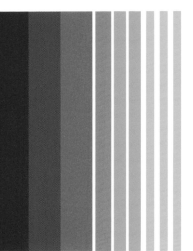

After climbing out of his battered machine and collecting himself, Busch headed for Victory Lane to congratulate the winner... "That was the coolest finish that I've ever seen and I'm glad that I was a part of it."

chances for victory ended with lug-nut mishaps on pit road. Jeff Gordon moved to the front and led for 78 laps but was forced to retire after his car caromed off Elliott Sadler's and hit the second-turn wall. Busch, with the power steering on his car going-going-gone, was the benefactor of the accident, slipping into a lead that he would hold for the next twenty-one laps.

At the same time, Ricky Craven had almost completed his charge to the front from the thirty-first starting spot, and with only twenty-two laps remaining his orange-and-white Tide Pontiac was stalking the back bumper of Busch's Taurus. Craven gained ground in each of the next twenty laps, pulling even on two occasions.

With two laps remaining Craven tried to take the lead by going low in Turn 1, but on his worn tires slid into Busch, who scraped the wall. Craven then skated

Craven celebrates after his big win.

up the track in front of Busch. As both drivers regained control Busch tapped Craven on the rear bumper, went low, and retook the lead. "All of a sudden I found him in front," Craven said. "Now how the hell did that happen?"

Busch tried to protect his position; Craven muscled forward and banged door-to-door with Busch down the homestretch. Neither driver backed off, neither driver flinched. And for the first time in a long while, a race was decided by a driver's nerve, not an over-engineered car.

The electronic timing system caught it perfectly: Craven by an inch. Maybe two. "I don't know how I saved it, I don't know how he saved it," Craven said after winning for the second time in his career. The right side of his Pontiac was mashed flat; the left side

of Busch's Ford was hammered beyond recognition. It was a finish for the ages, and one that will never be forgotten by 55,000 breathless fans, an astonished national television audience, and especially by two courageous NASCAR drivers.

After climbing out of his battered machine and collecting himself, Busch headed for Victory Lane to congratulate the winner. "I can't wait to see him, I'll certainly slap him a high-five and we'll share a couple beers later on," said Busch. "That was the coolest finish that I've ever seen and I'm glad that I was a part of it."

An astonished Craven also shared that remarkable sentiment. "I'll be sixty-five years old, sitting on the porch with my wife up on Moosehead Lake," he said, "and I'll tell this story a hundred thousand times."

2001 Atlanta: "This One's for Dale"
• • • • • • • • • •

There was no way for Kevin Harvick to fly under the radar with this.

Think of an icon, the heart and soul of one of America's most popular sports. Then imagine something bigger, and double it. At that point you're just beginning to get close to Dale Earnhardt's impact on and importance to NASCAR and the NASCAR family.

So when the unthinkable happened—when Dale Earnhardt was killed in a last-lap crash during the 2001 Daytona 500—it set in motion an unlikely series of events that would impact everyone connected with the sport. No one more than a twenty-five-year-old from Bakersfield, California.

A simple press release from Richard Childress Racing during the week following that fateful Daytona 500 said it all: "NASCAR Busch Series driver Kevin Harvick will move up to the Winston Cup Series."

Harvick was an intense and at the same time affable up-and-comer at RCR who hoped to build on the credentials he'd earned the previous season, when he won Busch Series Rookie of the Year honors. The 2001

plan was for him to run another full Busch season, but in the days following Earnhardt's death, Childress recalled, "Harvick came to me and said he'd do whatever he could to help the race team." At that moment, it meant getting behind the wheel of the most famous car in motor sports.

Out of respect for Earnhardt, and in hopes of making Harvick's challenge a little less stressful, the team changed the black number 3 to a white number 29 before Harvick's first race. He finished a very respectable fourteenth at Rockingham, and a week later Harvick came home an astounding eighth in Las Vegas.

But the best was yet to come.

NASCAR's traveling show rolled into Atlanta for the fourth race of the season, and Harvick posted the best qualifying effort of his brief Cup career: he would start fifth in the Cracker Barrel 500. The Goodwrench Chevy stayed in or near the top ten for the first 300 laps and then, to the surprise of everyone—or maybe to the surprise of no one—began to move even closer to the front of the pack. "There was somebody in the passenger seat making the car go a lot better than I was," Harvick explained later. "I felt somebody tapping me on the shoulder with about ten laps to go and saying, 'You'd better get going if you want to win this race.'"

As the NASCAR community held its collective breath, Harvick pulled off the only thing that could really begin the healing process: an Earnhardt-style three-wide pass for the lead, followed by an electrifying fender-

to-fender homestretch sprint with Jeff Gordon, and crowned with a gratifying victory by just 0.006 seconds.

"This one's for Dale," said the teary-eyed rookie. "Someone was watching over us today."

Kevin Harvick in the #29 Monte Carlo celebrates by doing donuts after winning the Winston Cup Cracker Barrel 500 at Atlanta Motorspeedway in Hampton, Georgia.

1993 Talladega: Earnhardt and Irvan

● ● ● ● ● ● ● ● ●

The 1993 NASCAR Winston Cup season had not, to put it mildly, gotten off to a great start.

Alan Kulwicki, the previous year's series champion who captured the hearts and imaginations of the NASCAR family with an impossibly low-budget run to the title, was killed in a plane crash during the sixth week of the season on his way to the spring race at Bristol International Speedway. Three months after that Davey Allison died when the helicopter he was piloting slammed into the infield at Talladega.

Just twelve days later, under the nearly crippling 100-degree September heat at that same Alabama track, the drivers, crews, and fans assembled to say a final goodbye to Allison and to run another race, one ironically named the DieHard 500.

Dale Earnhardt had been on fire over the previous two months of the '93 season: four victories in seven races. Up-and-coming new kid on the block Ernie Irvan, who made his Cup debut six years earlier in a Monte Carlo sponsored by, believe it or not, Dale Earnhardt Chevrolet, convincingly won the Talladega race in May and was expected to challenge his former benefactor.

In a race that would be described in later newspaper reports as "terrifying" and "wildly violent," the first of five caution flags flew when Robby Gordon, in the Robert Yates Racing Thunderbird formerly driven by Davey Allison, spun and crashed on Lap 56. The day's worst incident involved Stanley Smith, a journeyman driver from Chelsea, Alabama. He was sandwiched in a four-car collision on the 70th lap and helicoptered to the same medical center in Birmingham where Allison had died of head injuries two weeks earlier.

It came as a surprise to no one that when the white flag waved after 187 laps there were five cars in contention and the outcome of the race was still very much up for grabs. Earnhardt was in front of Kyle Petty by a car length, with Irvan, Dale Jarrett, and Mark Martin bunched close behind in a 185 mph knot. After the first turn Petty dove to the bottom groove into the lead. Then exiting Turn 2 Irvan drove low and went to the front past Earnhardt and Petty. In the third and final curve, Earnhardt caught Irvan and they ran side by side until Earnhardt nosed ahead to win by six inches.

"It was an all-day game," said Earnhardt, comparing the race to a high-speed chess match. "We made the last move and beat 'em."

1959 Daytona 500: The First Photo Finish

• • • • • • • • • •

I believe stock-car racing can become a nationally recognized sport by having a national points standing which will embrace the majority of large stock-car events. We do not know how big it can be if it's handled properly.
—NASCAR founder Bill France, 1947

As NASCAR's traveling show zigzagged in its infancy across the Southeast on mainly quarter- and half-mile dirt tracks, Bill France envisioned a *superspeedway* that would be the centerpiece of his developing NASCAR series. Construction crews broke ground at Daytona in 1957—its high-banked 2.5 miles nearly twice the size of Darlington, the biggest existing track on the circuit—and two years later it was ready for the green flag to fall.

The inaugural Daytona 500 took place on February 22, 1959, and the capacity crowd of 41,000 fans along with the fifty-nine drivers were suitably awed by the sheer magnitude of the new track. "I came through the tunnel and there were only two buildings," said Richard Petty, recalling his first experience at the speedway. "There was one road in and one road out. For a twenty-one-year-old kid who'd never seen anything like it, it seemed like it was ten miles to the other corner. It was more awesome than you'd believe." (The Man Who Would Be King finished fifty-seventh after being forced out of the race with mechanical problems after only eight laps.)

His father, Lee, was one of the acknowledged stars of the fledgling race series, having won the champi-

onship in 1954 and again four years later. And when he showed up with a brand-new car to race—a '59 Oldsmobile Super 88—all eyes were on him. But someone forgot to mention it to Johnny Beauchamp, a journeyman who would run just twenty-three races during his five seasons at NASCAR's top level.

The two had broken away from the rest of the field

Johnny Beauchamp (73), driving a 1959 Thunderbird, and Lee Petty (42), driving an Oldsmobile, were neck and neck on the last lap of the 500-mile late stock car and convertible race over the Daytona International Speedway here February 22, 1959, but Petty nosed out Beauchamp at the finish line. The average speed for the race was 135.521 miles per hour.

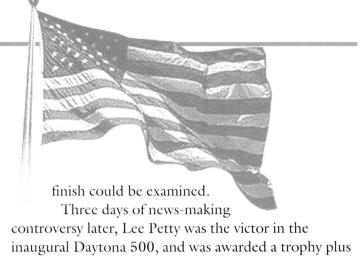

and swapped the lead over the final 30 laps. Petty took over on Lap 197 and led until the white flag, when Beauchamp moved his '59 Thunderbird even with Petty. Along with the lapped car of Joe Weatherly, it was a three-wide, side-by-side-by-side finish.

Both drivers claimed victory. Officials were inclined to think, but weren't a hundred percent positive, that Beauchamp had won. Petty lodged a protest, and NASCAR president Bill France decided to delay declaring a winner until photographs and newsreels of the finish could be examined.

Three days of news-making controversy later, Lee Petty was the victor in the inaugural Daytona 500, and was awarded a trophy plus the winner's check in the amount of $19,050.

1984 Talladega: Cale Yarborough
Barely Captures Eightieth Victory

• • • • • • • • •

Cale Yarborough was named by a panel of experts as one of NASCAR's 50 Greatest Drivers and he's fifth (behind Petty, Pearson, Allison, and Waltrip) on the all-time victories list. He's also a member of the International Motorsports Hall of Fame. But when asked, the intense driver from Timmonsville, South Carolina, doesn't hesitate to single out the 1984 Winston 500.

"It was the wildest race I have ever been in."

High-speed madness was part of the equation even before the cars began powering around the 2.66-mile, 33-degree-banked Talladega tri-oval, which was known then as Alabama International Motor Speedway. In the pre-restrictor-plate days of unlimited fire-breathing NASCAR horsepower, a record eight drivers qualified at more than 200 mph—the fastest stock car field in history—with Yarborough on the pole in a then-record of 202.692 mph.

And when the race began, it seemed even faster.

The tremendously competitive contest went thirty-nine flat-out, foot-on-the-floor, white-knuckles-on-the-steering-wheel laps before the caution flag was waved for debris on the track. At that point the field was *averaging* a blazing 193.161 mph. The pace did eventually slow due to the four yellow flags (another for debris, and when Geoff Bodine and Dale Earnhardt smacked the wall a few laps apart, both coincidentally in the fourth turn). But the competitive nature of the race never waned. There were a record seventy-five lead changes among thirteen drivers, including Yarborough and co-legends Richard Petty, Bobby Allison, Buddy Baker, Dale Earnhardt, Bill Elliott, David Pearson, and Benny Parsons.

Resting against his Hardee's-sponsored Chevrolet Monte Carlo SS, Cale Yarborough proudly holds up his first place trophy for the 1984 Winston 500. It was Yarborough's 80th victory, a landmark he captured at what was then known as the Alabama International Motor Speedway.

Cale's car—a Hardee's-sponsored Chevrolet Monte Carlo SS prepared by Waddell Wilson, the mechanical mastermind and acknowledged guru of high-speed engine wizardry—was certainly one of the stronger cars, if not the class of the field. However, there was one slight problem: his orange-and-white hot rod was running dangerously low on gas. Yarborough conserved his dwindling fuel by tucking in behind race leader Harry Gant on the 175th of 188 laps. But on the final circuit Yarborough combined horsepower, high-speed aerodynamics, and sheer guts to drive past Gant's Buick on the long backstretch for the seventy-fifth and final lead change. But even then he wasn't in the clear for the win.

"I heard my engine sputter and begin to die on the last turn. I had to pump it to get it to go again," said Yarborough. After reviving the engine, the three-time Cup champion stayed just ahead of Gant and went on to capture the eightieth victory of his NASCAR career.

In the pre-restrictor plate days of unlimited fire-breathing NASCAR horsepower, a record eight drivers qualified at more than 200 mph—the fastest stock car field in history— with Yarborough on the pole in a then-record of 202.692 mph.

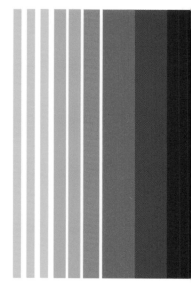

Following Gant, the next seven cars crossed the finish line just 0.33 of a second apart.

1991 Michigan: Jarrett and Allison in a Ford Shootout

• • • • • • • • •

Everywhere Dale Jarrett went, he was asked the same old question: *When are you going to win?* His stretch of 128 Cup races—almost four full seasons—without seeing the checkered flag really *was* a long time. And each week the pressure seemed to grow. Such is the curse of following a successful father—two-time series champion Ned Jarrett—into the family business.

Davey Allison, to some degree, also knew that same "son of" pressure. He was a rising star on the Cup circuit, a high-flying winner of eleven races in his young, full-of-promise career. But he also had championship shoes to fill: his father, Bobby Allison, was the 1983 series king, and was in fact still an active driver. So naturally, the inevitable father-son comparisons happened pretty much every week, with the late-summer contest on the Michigan International Speedway's two-mile D-shaped oval the next opportunity for evaluation and scrutiny.

But at the end of the 200-lap shootout the crowd was on its feet, 90,000 strong, cheering in unison for the dramatic duel of second-generation drivers they had just witnessed.

The younger Allison seemed unbeatable that day. He had dominated the Michigan race in June and appeared to be on his way to repeating the same formula. The 61 laps he led were the most by any driver. But Jarrett kept the Citgo Ford in contention on the track, and his crew kept the Thunderbird close during every pit stop.

Allison was in control with a comfortable lead over Mark Martin and Harry Gant, with Jarrett a car length behind in fourth, when the caution flag flew on Lap 187 for debris on the track. The leaders all needed a splash of fuel to make it to the finish, and everyone also got new tires. Everyone except Jarrett, who pulled out at the head of the pack.

The green flag waved on Lap 192 and the final nine laps saw Allison, who came out of the pits in fourth,

move up to challenge his fellow Thunderbird driver. On Lap 199, Allison got up alongside Jarrett and put the nose of his car ahead at the line to lead the penultimate lap. But Jarrett did not back off and they remained side by side over the last circuit. In the final 200 yards, Jarrett pulled even and then got the nose of his car out front in the last split second of the race.

After 400 miles, Jarrett had beaten Davey Allison by a scant eight inches in a fender-banging, door-rubbing, nail-biting Ford shootout. It was the closest finish in the history of the twenty-three-year-old Michigan track and prompted Jarrett to say after the race, "I thought it was maybe even a little closer than that."

2004 Texas: Sadler and Kahne's Wheel-to-Wheel Finish
• • • • • • • • •

The race at Texas Motor Speedway on April 4, 2004, was characterized by many in the media and in the grandstands as not particularly exciting, downright boring according to some accounts. The 1.5-mile quad oval is one of the so-called cookie-cutter tracks on the NASCAR circuit, very similar to Charlotte, Las Vegas, and Atlanta. The racing is always fast, but sometimes the banked asphalt resembles a parade route instead of a racetrack.

But take another look at that race date. The 04-04-04 rolled up like winning numbers on the NASCAR Cup slot machine, and the 200,000-plus fans in attendance hit the jackpot with a dazzling finish.

Bobby Labonte, the 2000 series champion, led the field to the green flag from his pole position, but was passed before the end of the first lap by Bill Elliott. Following a Lap 18 caution for the minor skirmish between Casey Mears and Jeff Gordon, the field settled down and almost appeared to be circling the track in a choreographed formation, with the exception of the bright red number 9 Dodge of Kasey Kahne.

The rookie sensation from Enumclaw, Washington, started the race in third but got shuffled back during the

first pit stop. From there, it was a not-so-slow march through the field to take the lead on Lap 49 from fellow Dodge driver Sterling Marlin. Kahne's car was a rocket and he dominated the Samsung/Radio Shack 500, leading six times for 148 laps. Not that any of this was a great surprise; he had already notched two very close second-place finishes in the season's first six races.

But there is one very important ingredient that usually factors into who wins a race and who doesn't: luck. Elliott Sadler had it and Kasey Kahne didn't. And that turned out to be the story.

Kahne, in the lead and in command, made what was supposed to be a routine green-flag pit stop. But Ward Burton's brush with the wall brought out the yellow flag on Lap 267 and pinned Kahne a lap down. Sadler, on the other hand, was in a small group that had not yet pitted. He came out in second place behind Jeff Gordon.

Sadler's good fortune continued when Gordon's momentary electrical glitch allowed the M&M's Taurus to slip by into the lead. Kahne's furious chase put him on Sadler's bumper, and the two roared out of the final turn almost wheel to wheel. But at the finish line it was Sadler, winning by a scant 0.028 of a second.

"If Kasey had two hundred more feet, he would have gotten me," Sadler conceded after the race.

Elliot Sadler (38) just beats Kasey Kahne (9) to the checkered flag to win the NASCAR Samsung/Radio Shack 500 at the Texas Motor Speedway, Fort Worth, on Sunday, April 4, 2004.

1992 Points Race: Kulwicki Takes the Cup on Fumes

• • • • • • • • • •

There was a time when "college degree in mechanical engineering" and "NASCAR driver" were rarely if ever found in the same sentence. But University of Wisconsin graduate Alan Kulwicki always had his own way of getting things done.

After establishing his racing credentials in the Midwest-based American Speed Association, Kulwicki packed his belongings into his truck and made the move to North Carolina in 1986. There he set up shop for his shot at the big time, not in the traditional manner of driving someone else's car but by creating a team of his own. Alan Kulwicki Racing operated on a shoestring budget: He used engineering know-how and gritty determination to keep his team inching forward. Following the first win three years later, Kulwicki took NASCAR celebrations in an entirely new direction with his wrong-way-around-the-track "Polish victory lap."

By the 1992 season Kulwicki's team was running with the leaders on a weekly basis. In fact, with five races remaining on the schedule he was one of five drivers who still had a mathematical chance to catch points leader Bill Elliott and win the Cup championship. Of course, being underfunded *and* 191 points behind a veteran driver who had won the championship in 1988, it was decidedly a long shot.

Over the next three races Elliott, his main challenger Davey Allison, and Kulwicki chased points and each other around the tracks at North Wilkesboro, Charlotte, and Rockingham, but Elliott still held comfortable leads over both his rivals. A second championship seemed within Elliott's grasp if everything followed form in the season's penultimate race a week later in Phoenix.

But as so often it goes in sports, it turned out to be a big if. The breaks instead went against Elliott: a cracked cylinder head took him

Alan Kulwicki holds up the Winston Cup trophy at Atlanta Raceway after winning the 1992 Championship.

out early. Allison won and Kulwicki raced to a fourth-place finish. As the teams headed to Atlanta for the final race the standings had shifted dramatically: Allison led Kulwicki by 30, with Elliott in third just 10 points back.

As the November race progressed, Davey was running well and appeared to be in control of his destiny; the sixth-place finish he needed to clinch the Cup title was well within his reach. But on Lap 256 Ernie Irvan blew a tire and took Allison out of the race and the championship chase. Kulwicki then made his chancy strategic move: he risked running out of gas by staying on the track when Elliott pitted for fuel; but by remaining out and leading one more lap than Elliott, Kulwicki earned five bonus points by leading the most laps in the contest. His "Underbird"—a Thunderbird with the T and the H removed as a nod to their lack of funding—crossed the finish line in second, just behind Elliott. Kulwicki's 10-point cushion won him the 1992 NASCAR Cup Series championship—and the million dollars—by one of the narrowest margins in NASCAR history.

1992 Winston: Davey Allison Spins Across the Finish Line

• • • • • • • • •

"I remember the whole race Saturday night till I crossed the finish line, then the lights went out."

You'll have to forgive Davey Allison for using a metaphor that may have seemed slightly confusing to spectators thrilled out of their seats with the action during the 1992 Winston all-star race. Charlotte Motor Speedway general manager Humpy Wheeler had just ponied up $1.7 million for a lighting system, and the Saturday night crowd of 135,500 was at that time the largest to witness a nighttime sporting event.

But it wasn't those lights Allison was talking about.

The top drivers from the NASCAR Cup ranks were tested in individual segments of thirty, thirty, and ten laps. In a new twist to the all-star format, the fans were polled and voted by a two-to-one margin to invert the finish of that opening race for the start of the second thirty laps, and that's where the excitement began. First-segment front-runners Allison, Kyle Petty, and Rusty Wallace made electrifying charges back through the field to the front.

But in the finest tradition of Saturday night racing, the drivers saved their best for the final ten-lap sprint.

The Pontiac, Chevy, and Ford of Kyle Petty, Dale Earnhardt, and Davey Allison were battling for the lead—and the $200,000 winner's share—going into the final turn. "I saw Kyle and Dale Earnhardt go at it in Turn 3 the last lap, and I thought, 'We'll win this race if I can miss the wreck,'" Allison would recall when the dust had finally settled. "Dale got sideways in Turn 4, Kyle had to lift a little, and that gave me a shot at him."

But Allison collided with Petty—or vice versa—and was sent spinning, at 170 mph and driver's side first, into the outside wall...but *not* before he had crossed the finish line. Car and driver drifted limply to the infield grass as the fans stood in silence. Allison was cut out of his mangled car and airlifted to a local hospital. The crash cost him a concussion (which momentarily knocked him senseless), bruised knees and shoulders, and a bruised lung. But it was Davey Allison's victory. And he was back behind the wheel a week later for the longest race of the Cup season, the Coca-Cola 600.

"I know Kyle didn't do it on purpose," Allison said. "We've stood around and laughed about it. There are no hard feelings. It was just close racing."

Davey Allison leads a pack of five cars on the final lap of the Winston 500 at the Talladega Superspeedway May 3, 1992. Behind Allison are Dale Earnhardt *(middle left)*, Bill Elliott *(middle right)*, Ernie Irvan, *(back left)* and Sterling Marlin. Allison went on to win the race.

Carl Edwards, driver of the #99 Roush Racing Ford, performs a back flip as crew members look on after winning the NASCAR Nextel Cup Series Bass Pro Shops MBNA 500 on October 30, 2005 at Atlanta Motor Speedway in Hampton, Georgia.

2005 Atlanta: Carl Edwards Flips for His Wins

• • • • • • • • •

Moving full-time behind the wheel of a Roush Ford for the 2005 Nextel Cup season, an easygoing twenty-six-year-old second-generation rookie driver from Columbia, Missouri, named Carl Edwards immediately understood the harsh realities of racing: every driver at the top of the pyramid has a star-studded résumé, with a list of accolades, awards, and championships longer than the backstretch at Martinsville.

So...how *do* you distinguish yourself from the other big-name Cup drivers?

For starters, a dizzying display of skill, pinpoint car control, and NASCAR etiquette, coupled with twelfth-place, fifth-place, and fourteenth-place finishes in the first three races of the season, had been a great induction for Edwards to the most exclusive enclave of racing. It showed fellow drivers and fans that he had to be considered "one of the guys." But during a March weekend at Atlanta Motor Speedway for the fourth race of the 2005 season, Edwards added an entirely new flip to Cup racing and became one of *the* guys.

This new spin began on Saturday in the Busch race. Edwards started on the pole and piloted his Charter Communications Ford to the checkered flag ahead of three acknowledged Cup Series superstars: former champions Tony Stewart and Matt Kenseth, and 2005 series points leader Jimmie Johnson. It was his first Busch Series win. But after an abbreviated Victory Lane celebration, it was back to the business of being a Cup driver on the eve of another big race.

When the green flag fell for Sunday's Cup race at Atlanta Motor Speedway things got quickly out of hand. The forty-three cars were barely past the start-finish line when Casey Mears touched off a melee in Turn 2 that involved almost a quarter of the field, eliminating from contention two drivers who are always a threat to win at AMS: four-time series champion Jeff Gordon, and Bobby Labonte, who with six wins is the active driver with the most victories at that track.

From there things settled down—into a 190 mph battle between the dominant cars and crews of Jimmie Johnson and Greg Biffle. Between them they led 307 of the 335 laps. Edwards ran near or in the top five all day but only managed to lead nine laps. Included in that nine, though, was the most important one.

On the final circuit Edwards, in second, got a great run coming out of Turn 2 and pulled up on leader

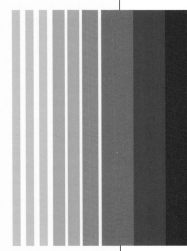

Edwards's charm, enthusiasm and neon smile illuminated the victory lane celebration, but the highlight came when he climbed to the window ledge of his green and white Ford and executed a spectacular backflip down to the track—and into the record book.

Johnson's back bumper. Johnson guided the Lowe's Chevy high through Turns 3 and 4, trying to block his challenger, but Edwards went even higher. He brushed the wall and the two cars touched just a few feet from the finish, but Edwards slipped by to win, after 500 miles of hard racing, by just 0.028 seconds.

Edwards's charm, enthusiasm, and neon smile illuminated the Victory Lane celebration, but the highlight came when he climbed to the window ledge of his green-and-white Ford and executed a spectacular backflip down to the track—and into the record book. With his second victory of the weekend, Carl Edwards became the only driver to win back-to-back Busch and Cup races at Atlanta and the only driver to do it in the same weekend.

Chapter Two
CINDERELLA MEN
The Unlikeliest Victories

*Demonstrating the talent that made
him a four-time NASCAR champ, Jeff Gordon
steadily clawed his way back, passing every car on
the track, once, twice, then three times.*

Derrike Cope's 1990 Daytona Surprise

● ● ● ● ● ● ● ● ● ●

The 1990 Daytona 500 is one of *the* legendary NASCAR races, in large part because of Derrike Cope's incredibly unlikely win, but above all because it was a crushing loss for the race leader and odds-on favorite, Dale Earnhardt.

In his previous fifteen years as a NASCAR driver, the Intimidator had won nearly every kind of competition run at Daytona International Speedway, be it a Busch Series race, an IROC race, a qualifying race, or an all-star race, twenty-nine victories in all. But the one that mattered—the Daytona 500—was coming to be known as Earnhardt's curse, and the events of the 1990 race cemented that superstition.

On the other hand, Derrike Cope hadn't been in NASCAR long enough to develop a reputation, let alone a curse. This was just the third Daytona 500 for the

thirty-one-year-old former college baseball player from little Spanaway, Washington, whose career was ended by a knee injury. Cope was so green he had yet to be included in NASCAR's media guide. But on February 18, 1990, the NASCAR *world* took notice of him.

As the 1990 edition of the Great American Race

wound down, it truly looked likded Dale Earnhardt's drought was finally over. His famous black number 3 GM Goodwrench Chevy dominated 155 of the race's 200 laps. At one point, Earnhardt led by 39 seconds, nearly three-quarters of a lap. But then, with eight laps to go, Geoff Bodine's spin brought out the day's third

caution flag and bunched up the field for a five-lap dash to the checkered flag.

Earnhardt hit the pits for left-side tires while Cope stayed out on the raceway. When the caution flag lifted, Cope had moved into first place, but Earnhardt quickly took it back. "Nobody was going to catch me until that caution came out," Dale insisted after the race. "Even after that, I had no trouble driving by Derrike on the restart. The race was still mine."

With 50 laps to go, a reporter interviewed Rusty Wallace's engine builder, Harold Elliott, who told him "I think the only way anybody will beat Dale Earnhardt today is to shoot his tires out."

Derrike Cope would have been the first to agree. Though he had hung around the front-runners all day, it was enough of a battle keeping his car on the track. "I was really fighting to hold on to second place," Cope remembers. "My car was very loose."

Going into the last lap, Earnhardt's crew and family were jubilant. With Dale less than a mile from the finish line, a CBS Sports TV camera caught his wife holding their daughter and listening intently to the scanner in the family's motor home. But the celebrating would prove to be premature.

Thundering into the last turn of the last lap, a small piece of metal debris from Ricky Rudd's blown bell-housing chomped on Dale Earnhardt's right rear tire. "It went [flat] right in front of the chicken-bone grandstands on the backstretch," Earnhardt said after the race. "I heard it hit the bottom of the car, and then it hit the tire and the tire went." All Dale could do was steer the car to the top of the track and stay out of everyone's way. His twelfth trip to Daytona would not change his luck.

Meanwhile, the unlikeliest and luckiest man in NASCAR zoomed into the lead. "When I saw what was happening to Dale, I just turned that baby left," Cope said. "I saw a hole and had my foot on the floor. I knew at that point we had the thing won. I wasn't going to let anybody beat me, even if I had to block the track all the way to the checkers."

Cope was able to hold off Terry Labonte for the

last third of a lap and registered one of the biggest upsets in the history of the 500.

After the race, CBS cut back to the Earnhardts' motor home to find both his wife and daughter in tears. The number 3 crew was dazed by the bad luck.

Cope told reporters: "I know you guys are stunned. So am I. Something like this usually comes just once in a lifetime."

Derrike Cope was right about that. In the many seasons since, he has only scored one more #1, a victory that same year at Dover. But until the end of time, he will be referred to as "Daytona 500 winner Derrike Cope."

Dale Earnhardt? After the race, he was emotionally drained, but stoic. "This has been the biggest buildup and biggest letdown I've ever had in racing," he said. "There's nothing you can do about it, either. You can't kick the car and cry and pout and lay down and squall and bawl. You've got to take it and walk on."

Walk on Dale did—and eight years later he finally won the Daytona 500—on his twentieth try. The tire

that cost him the race? Earnhardt and team owner Richard Childress took it back to North Carolina and nailed it over the door to the race shop, where it served as a reminder that in NASCAR, no race is truly over until you see the checkered flag.

Kyle Petty: The First Third-Generation Cup Victory

• • • • • • • • •

Despite being born into one of motor racing's premier dynasties, it was not Kyle Petty's intention to follow his grandfather, Lee, and his father, Richard, into the family trade. Growing up, Kyle excelled in sports. In fact, the six-foot-two athlete was offered college scholarships in both football and baseball. Some say he even sang well enough to have a pretty decent music career.

But Kyle was a Petty; the fluid running through his veins was a fifty-fifty mix of blood and racing fuel. So in 1979, at just nineteen, Kyle entered his first major stock car race, a 200-mile ARCA event at Daytona International Speedway. The precocious teenager won and soon after became his father's Cup series teammate competing under the Petty Enterprises banner. That year, Richard won the series championship and Kyle collected his first top ten finish. The teaming lasted

until 1985, when Kyle moved out from under the long shadow of King Richard to join the legendary Wood Brothers racing team. The change paid off royally a year later in Richmond, Virginia.

Dale Earnhardt was clearly in charge that day, leading 299 laps of the 400-lap 1986 Miller 400. Darrell Waltrip stayed in contention and in fact bumped and banged Chevys around the three-quarter-mile oval all day, but with just three laps to go, it looked like Dale would be the one celebrating in Victory Lane.

With the finish line just a couple of miles away, Waltrip managed to squeeze by Earnhardt in Turn 3. Dale quickly tried to take the lead back but ran out of room and clipped DW's rear quarter panel, sending the cars up into the guardrail, out of contention and of the race, and taking Geoff Bodine and Joe Ruttman, in third and fourth, with them. While the top four were

busy rearranging each other's sheet metal, Kyle Petty dropped underneath, grabbed the lead and, a couple of laps later, his first NASCAR Cup checkered flag.

Kyle gives much of the credit for the win to the hardworking Wood Brothers pit crew. "We had a top five car and we were there all day long....[Earnhardt and Waltrip] got in the wreck and we dodged it, but...Eddie [Wood] and everybody in the pits put us in position. We'd come in running fourth or fifth and go out running second or third. I'd lose a couple of positions because of inexperience on the racetrack, but they kept...putting me in position to win and then when trouble broke loose we were in the right place at the right time."

That highly unexpected victory made Kyle Petty the first third-generation driver to win a Cup event.

Bobby Labonte Snatches the Last Winston Cup

● ● ● ● ● ● ● ● ●

The thirty-sixth and final race of the 2003 season, at Homestead-Miami Speedway, marked the end of an era. After thirty-three years NASCAR was changing sponsors from Winston to Nextel. As the France family moved from tobacco to telephones, they continued their goal of repositioning the sport for the twenty-first century.

Homestead-Miami had also been spruced up for the new millennium. Never one of the drivers' favorite tracks, the formerly flat 1.5-mile oval had been resurfaced and given state-of-the-art "progressive" banking. At first the new configuration seemed to be a blessing as lap times climbed exponentially. Later it proved to be a curse, eating up right front tires and shredding right rears.

NASCAR veteran Bill Elliott came into the race on a roll. That season he'd been "Mr. Consistency," competing in all but one race and finishing in the top ten eleven times. Just the week before he had won the Pop Secret 400, outracing points leaders Matt Kenseth and Jimmie Johnson. On the other hand, the 2000 Cup champion, Bobby Labonte, was not on a roll. He hadn't won since the fourth race of the season, a dry spell of eight long months.

For 189 of the 267 laps Elliott and his dominant Dodge led a caution-riddled race. It seemed like a lock: Million-Dollar Bill would close out the 2003 season in the winner's circle. At the other end of the pack, Bobby Labonte started poorly but worked his way through the field. On Lap 265 he trailed Elliott in second but still held little hope. "With two [laps] to go, I said, 'I want this win more than he does, maybe, but his car is really good right now.' There's no way, unless something happened, that I was going to pass him."

With victory less than 1,000 yards away, Homestead nibbled on Bill Elliott's right rear tire and it began to lose pressure. To Labonte, it was like an early Christmas. "He [Elliott] just started wiggling," Bobby remembers. "And I just started screaming on the radio. It was a gift. It was way cool for us to win a race. We've been a long time without it, since Atlanta, so we just had a good day...and we had a lot of fun."

For Bobby Labonte, and for NASCAR, it was an exciting way to end the 2003 Winston Cup season and ignite the Nextel Cup Series.

Mark Martin's Lap Lapse at Bristol 1994

● ● ● ● ● ● ● ● ● ●

If NASCAR drivers were in a race for "Most Embarrassing Moment," Mark Martin's unbelievable mental lapse in the 1994 Busch Series race at Bristol would finish five laps ahead of the pack.

Except for that improbable event, it had been a terrific season for Martin. That year, he was barking up Dale Earnhardt's tailpipe for the Cup championship and would eventually finish second to the Intimidator.

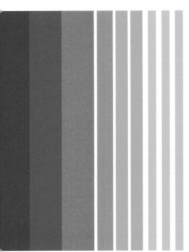

For reasons only Martin himself can explain, he steered the Winn-Dixie Ford out of Turn 4, intending to motor into Victory Lane. The problem was the race wasn't over. Martin had pulled off the track a lap short.

He started thirty-one Cup races and won a pair. He started fifteen Busch Series races and won three. After the season Martin would bank over $1.6 million in combined winnings.

Former national go-kart champion David Green was having a pretty great year as well. Driving in the Busch Series for his friend and mentor Bobby Labonte, Green finished in the top five ten times, won the BGN championship, and pulled in a career-high $218,664 in prize money. After finishing second to Jeff Gordon in the 1991 Rookie of the Year competition, Green was proving he was a big-league pilot to be reckoned with.

Also to be reckoned with was the Bristol International Raceway track. At just over a half-mile long, it's one of NASCAR's shortest tracks, and the

36-degree-banked turns are the circuit's steepest. Those factors make the races terrific to watch for the fans and a serious challenge for the racers on the concrete. David Green has said that driving there is like "flying a fighter jet in a gymnasium," and in fact, Bristol bills itself as the "World's Fastest Half-Mile."

But the racers were nowhere near that tempo on April 9, 1994; they were in fact coasting under a yellow caution flag on Lap 249 of 250. Mark Martin was leading, a certain winner with nothing more complicated to do than follow the pace car around the track and collect $22,000.

For reasons only Martin himself can explain, he steered the Winn-Dixie Ford out of Turn 4, intending to motor into Victory Lane. The problem was the race wasn't over. Martin had pulled off the track a lap short.

David Green cruised across the finish line in his Slim Jim Chevy, scoring his only win of 1994. Martin ended up finishing eleventh, done in by a mental mistake that cost him a win and over $18,000 in prize money.

Jeremy Mayfield Ends His Four-Year Winless Streak

● ● ● ● ● ● ● ● ●

In 2004, hoping to amp up the excitement of their premier series, NASCAR instituted a new method to determine the Cup winner. In the new Chase for the Championship only the top ten points leaders after the first twenty-six races are eligible to compete for the Cup. Each qualifier enters the ten-race Chase separated by just five points per position; the first-place driver starts with 5,050 points, the second-place driver with 5,045 points, and so on down the line. Being separated by so few points gives every top ten driver a good shot at the title.

The new plan proved to be an effective one. On September 12, 2004, when the last race of the regular season was run at Richmond, seven of the ten Chase for the Championship spots were filled. Eight drivers had a mathematical shot at the three remaining slots, guaranteeing that the competition would be fierce and the fans would witness a great race.

Among the eight hopefuls was thirty-five-year-old Jeremy Mayfield. The 1993 ARCA Rookie of the Year was in fourteenth place and needed an amazing race, a top finish, and a bunch of luck (something he'd been very short on) to make the Chase. The fact that Jeremy hadn't visited Victory Lane in over four years—143 races—made him the darkest of dark horses.

With so much at stake, some of the drivers really pushed it to the limit. One of those was Casey Mears. Jimmie Johnson, the series points leader, said Mears did something on the track to infuriate Jimmy Spencer, and Spencer was determined to make him pay. "[Spencer] was chasing [Mears] from the bottom of the racetrack all the way up to the marbles trying to wreck him....[It was] desperate guys doing desperate things." On Lap 180, Spencer finally tagged Mears and the result was a massive ten-car pileup that took Johnson and several others out of the race.

Brushing his bad luck and the desperate drivers aside, Jeremy Mayfield led for 151 laps, driving hard, staying away from trouble, and, most importantly, stopping for fuel on the right schedule. With eight laps to go Kurt Busch was leading the race, but his team had miscalculated the fuel load. He ran out of gas and handed the lead to a shocked Mayfield.

"I couldn't believe it," Jeremy said after the race.

Jeremy Mayfield (19) passes Dale Earnhardt Jr. (8) in turn 4 at Richmond International Raceway in Richmond, Virginia, Saturday, September 11, 2004. Mayfield won the NASCAR Chevy Rock & Roll 400 and moved into the top 10 in points.

"The way my luck's been I thought there's no way in hell [Busch] is going to run out of gas...all of a sudden he ran out, and I was like, 'This can't be true. Now it's my turn to either cut a tire or hit the wall or something.' "

But this time Jeremy's luck held, ending his four-year drought, vaulting him from number fourteen to number nine in the standings and supplying the appropriate first big moment for the inaugural Chase for the Championship.

The Little Black Taxi That Could

• • • • • • • • •

In the history of NASCAR, Johnny Mantz's ride in the 1950 Darlington 500 is the odds-on favorite to win as Unlikeliest Race Car Ever to Finish First. In fact, in the days leading up to the event, Mantz's entry wasn't a race car at all. It was NASCAR founder Bill France's "Little Black Taxi," a boxy stock, six-cylinder, 97-horsepower Plymouth business coupe he and other race promoters bought to run errands around Darlington. It remained the Little Black Taxi until Mantz, lacking a ride, begged France to let him borrow the car for the race and slapped a set of numbers on it.

The 1950 Darlington 500 was notable for more than Mantz's unlikely victory. It was NASCAR's first 500-mile race, and the very first event held on a paved circuit. All previous races had been held on dirt tracks.

Johnny Mantz, whose nickname was "Madman Mantz," proved himself the opposite. He was a crafty competitor who had finished thirteenth and seventh in

Johnny Mantz's unlikely winner.

the two previous Indianapolis 500s. He had raced 500 miles on pavement and understood exactly what he'd need to do: run cautiously, conserving the little Plymouth, his fuel, and his tires. The heavy V-8 Cadillacs and Oldsmobiles, driving 80–90 mph on the banked oval, burned through and blew out tires at a startling rate. In fact, some teams actually ran out of tires during the race and were forced to beg, borrow, and buy tires off fans parked in the infield.

After starting forty-third—he was the slowest

qualifier of the seventy-five starters—Mantz circled the track on the apron, cruising at about 75 mph, the Plymouth sipping gas and tiptoeing on its tires, the tortoise to seventy-four hares. Now, about those tires. Legend has it Mantz was running truck tires—extra-hard rubber that lasted a lot longer than his competition's.

Richard Petty says they were actually racing tires. "At that point...I didn't even know that there was such an animal as a race tire," he remembers. "Mantz had them shipped down from his buddies in Akron, Ohio. They were the old five-rib Firestones that had been used on a couple cars at Indy....They had been built to stand high speeds, so they were probably better than the Sears Allstates that we had....Johnny was the only one that had anything that even resembled a real racing tire."

The race took an unbelievable 6 hours and 39 minutes to complete, during which Johnny Mantz and the Little Black Taxi rolled up a nine-lap lead on second-place Fireball Roberts. When NASCAR's first-ever 500 was in the books, it included two records that have yet to beaten: Mantz's starting position, forty-third, is the

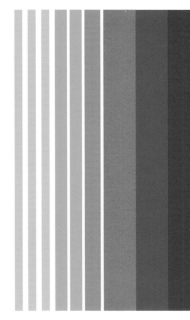

The heavy V-8 Cadillacs and Oldsmobiles, driving 80-90 mph on the banked oval, burned through and blew out tires at a startling rate. In fact, some teams actually ran out of tires during the race and were forced to beg, borrow and buy tires off fans parked in the infield.

farthest back anyone has begun a 500-mile race and won, and 351 is the most laps anyone has ever led a 500-mile race.

NASCAR's Newly Minted "Million-Dollar Bill"

● ● ● ● ● ● ● ● ●

In 1985, RJ Reynolds Tobacco, in an effort to get the most out of their investment in NASCAR, offered a $1 million bonus to any driver who won three of NASCAR's four "grand slam" events: Daytona, Talladega, Charlotte, and Darlington. This seemingly impossible task (no one had done it before) for (then) impossible money was called the "Winston Million," and Reynolds's gamble paid off handsomely.

Going into the Southern 500, Bill Elliott had already visited Victory Lane nine times that season, including a win at Daytona and an amazing come-from-behind victory at Talladega. Suddenly, that unattainable million seemed within reach. But at Charlotte, Elliott's brakes failed and he finished a disappointing eighteenth. This made the fourth event,

at Darlington, do or die, and the media was all over it.

According to NASCAR president Mike Helton, "A lot of eyes and ears were on Darlington for that race. It was one of this sport's milestones." The media coverage was unprecedented. *Sports Illustrated*, which had seemingly always looked down its nose at stock car racing, made "Awesome Bill from Dawsonville" their cover story, the first NASCAR driver so honored. Happily for everyone, the competition lived up to the hype.

Bill Elliott drove a conservative but masterful race. He ducked around accidents dead in front of him, maneuvered through fourteen cautions, and outlasted front-runners Dale Earnhardt and Harry Gant, who were knocked out by engine problems. As the race wound down, there was one driver who could scuttle Elliott's designs on the bonus: five-time Southern 500 winner Cale Yarborough. Elliott said, "I knew if I made one mistake, Cale would be right there to take advantage of it." It was a battle to the finish, but in the end, Yarborough was done in by a five-buck part. Late in the race his power steering belt let go and that was enough for Bill to beat him to the line by a razor slim six-tenths of a second.

Ironically, while the Winston Million helped make NASCAR and Bill Elliott household names, he ended up with a whole lot less than that. Team owner Harry Melling took the lion's share of the cash and the pit crew was amply rewarded. After the IRS extracted its cut, the newly christened "Million-Dollar Bill" pocketed only about $75,000.

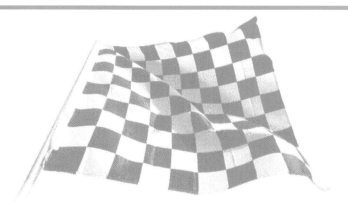

But that was okay with Elliott. "It changed the way people look at the sport and the respect they had for it," he explained. "But I don't think it changed my life....I wasn't racing for a million dollars, I was racing to win, same as always." Perhaps just as important to easygoing Bill Elliott was the Most Popular Driver award he won that year.

Tiny's Big Win at 1963 Daytona 500

• • • • • • • • • •

There was absolutely nothing tiny about DeWayne Lund. This six-foot-six, 300-pound hulk of an Iowan had one of the biggest smiles, the biggest personalities, and the biggest hearts in racing. Back in 1963, those attributes plus his hard-charging driving earned Tiny Lund the biggest win of his long career.

The story actually begins ten days before the 500 during Speedweeks. Marvin Panch, who'd already qualified the famed number 21 Wood Brothers Galaxie, was testing an experimental Ford-powered Maserati at Daytona, trying to win the $10,000 Bill France had put up for the first driver to run 180 mph. Panch was rocketing down the backstretch when the Maserati suddenly went airborne, crunched down on its side, and skidded to a stop upside down. With fire engulfing the engine compartment, Panch was trapped.

Fortunately, Tiny Lund and four other men were just coming out of a nearby tunnel and sprinted to the accident. As they tried to lift the burning Maserati off Panch, the fuel tank burst into flames, driving everyone back. They tried again. As the other four lifted the car, Tiny pulled Panch from the wreckage, saving his life and earning himself the Carnegie Medal for Heroism. At the hospital, doctors determined that Panch would survive his burns, but he certainly wouldn't drive in the 500. After a hospital-room conference, Marvin and the Woods graciously offered Tiny, who'd come to Daytona without a ride, the chance to drive the number 21.

The 1963 Daytona 500 was won on gas and tire strategy and there was nobody better at that than the Wood Brothers. As the field narrowed, the competition for the lead came down to Fred Lorenzen, Ned Jarrett, and Lund. Lorenzen and Jarrett helped each other conserve fuel by drafting together. Tiny helped himself

save gas by slowing down in front of Jarrett and letting Jarrett's car "push" him around the track.

Incredibly, Lund's Ford ran the entire 500 miles on one set of tires. Glen Wood remembers, "Back then, tires had tread on them and...would stick better as a slick. As they got worn down, they were better than they were with full tread on them...so, we just kept checking them." They also kept an extremely close watch on their fuel consumption. The strategy gave them the confidence to pit just four times, one less than the others. After Jarrett and Lorenzen both ran out of gas in the final laps, Tiny still had fuel to burn.

While legend has it that Lund coasted under the checkered flag, his engine sputtering on fumes, Glen Wood disagrees. "He just imagined it, I guess. When we loaded the car onto the truck it still had fuel in it. It could have sputtered on the final turn and maybe he thought he was out of gas. But it hadn't sputtered all day."

Tiny Lund's career, and his life, ended tragically at Talladega in 1975. But his legend and his Cinderella victory at the 1963 Daytona 500 live on, a life lived extra large.

Jeff Gordon's Bittersweet Win at Martinsville 2005

● ● ● ● ● ● ● ● ●

If Jeff Gordon has proved anything since starting his NASCAR career in 1992, it is that you should never, *ever* count him out. As long as his spark plugs are firing and his car has four tires, he's going to be a contender. Gordon hammered that point home at Martinsville in 2005. Still, it was one of the most unlikely wins of his career.

Returning to Martinsville in April 2005 couldn't have been easy for Jeff and the rest of the Hendrick Motorsports team. Barely six months before, on October 24, 2004, ten team and family members were killed when the company plane, heading for Martinsville, went down in heavy fog. The victims included owner Rick Hendrick's son, his twin nieces, and his brother. This certainly wasn't the way one of the sport's most successful teams wanted to mark their twentieth year in racing.

Jeff Gordon started the next season on a high note, taking the checkers at the Daytona 500. But after that big win, his luck was mixed; engine troubles and an accident dropped him from first to twelfth in the Cup standings. So Martinsville was important to him for a lot of reasons.

The race was the kind of competition that track is famous for. This half-mile, paper-clip-shaped flat track has a single groove. Passing is an invitation to trouble and there is usually lots of banging and bumping and major tire trouble. During that April 10, 2005, race, every single one of the forty-three cars that started the race had some kind of damage.

Pole sitter Scott Riggs didn't even make it through Lap 1, and the race was marred by sixteen yellow flags, most caused by flat tires. On Lap 48, a loose wheel forced Jeff Gordon to pit, and by the time he reentered the race he was three laps down. It looked like he'd have to settle for a back-of-the-pack finish. But Gordon had another goal in mind and 400-plus laps to achieve it.

Demonstrating the talent that made him a four-time NASCAR champ, Jeff steadily clawed his way back, passing every car on the track, once, twice, then three times. On Lap 466, the number 24 DuPont Chevy grabbed the lead from Sterling Marlin and never surrendered it. This extraordinary come-from-behind win catapulted Jeff back into the top ten, from number twelve to number six, and gave him one of his most satisfying and heartfelt victories.

After the race, Gordon dedicated the bittersweet win to his missing comrades. "There is something special about this place," he said. "We lost so many incredible people out of this organization and racing community [the previous fall]. I think it is only fitting for us to get this victory. I know how much it means to Rick Hendrick and his family and all those other families. It means a lot to this race team."

Jeff Gordon makes his presence known.

Reversal of Fortune: The 1989 All-Star Challenge at Charlotte

● ● ● ● ● ● ● ● ●

The 1989 All-Star Challenge at Lowe's Motor Speedway (then the Charlotte Motor Speedway) turned two big careers upside down. In a split second a longtime villain was turned into an instant hero and a relatively unknown up-and-comer became one of NASCAR's most talked-about drivers.

> *The villain was Darrell Waltrip, a guy everyone loved to hate. Breaking in, Waltrip had the nerve to brag to one and all that he was going to whip everyone's heroes. Neither the fans nor the drivers appreciated that disrespectful attitude.*

The villain was Darrell Waltrip, a guy everyone loved to hate. Breaking in, Waltrip had the nerve to brag to one and all that he was going to whip everyone's heroes. Neither the fans nor the drivers appreciated that disrespectful attitude. Then when Waltrip actually went out and did it, the fans despised him all the more.

Several factors in the 1989 season helped DW reverse his bad-guy image. The fans became more receptive when he and his wife, Stevie, had their first child, and, after seventeen years of trying, he finally won the Daytona 500. The stage was set for Darrell's image change—all it would take was a push in the right direction. Russell "Rusty" Wallace, eager to make a name for himself, was more than happy to supply it. Literally.

"I was pretty much still an unknown, just one of the younger drivers who sort of blended into the crowd," Rusty explains. "I was just a short-track hotshot who'd...paid my dues and was starting to win races in the big league."

The race itself was nothing out of the ordinary, the most tense moment being Kyle Petty's nasty crash. With two laps to go, it looked certain that Darrell Waltrip's Tide-sponsored Chevrolet was in position to take home the $200,000 first-place prize. But Rusty Wallace wouldn't let Waltrip pocket the cash without one last shot.

"I finally caught him and...I stuck my nose under his left rear quarter panel and it started to push a little bit," Rusty remembers. "I was like, 'Man, don't lift. If you lift, you're screwed.' I never lifted and he started sliding and—bam!—went the quarter panel, and all hell broke loose."

Waltrip slid sideways into the infield, a maneuver forever after known as the "Tide Slide." Wallace won the race, but the battle had just begun. The fans and Waltrip were livid at Wallace's tactic. A fight broke out in the infield between the two drivers' crews as Darrell fumed, "It was an ugly, ugly win. I hope he chokes on the $200,000, that's all I can tell him."

In that split second at Charlotte, Darrell Waltrip became a good guy and Rusty Wallace earned a reputation. "Regardless of all the wins, top fives and top tens, the poles and the money," Wallace says, "that win was probably the single most monumental event in my career." That year, Rusty went on to win the Cup championship, and Darrell Waltrip won an honor that before had been practically unthinkable: he was voted by the fans as NASCAR's Most Popular Driver.

THE DOMINATORS

*Over the next 33 years, Richard Petty would compile
one of the most overwhelming records in stock car racing,
while collecting seven Grand National/Cup titles,
becoming the sport's most valuable and visible ambassador
and earning his rightful title, The King.*

Richard Petty: Long Live the King
(Richard Petty's Crowning Victory)

● ● ● ● ● ● ● ● ●

In all of sports there are very few records that stand as unattainable—records that will almost certainly never be broken. Among them are amazing feats like Wilt Chamberlain's 100-point game, Nolan Ryan's seven career no-hitters, and Jerry Rice's 22,895 career receiving yards.

When it comes to NASCAR, Richard Petty set two records that will *never* be touched. In 1967 he racked up an impossible twenty-seven Cup circuit wins (including a record ten in a row), and in 1984 he celebrated his 200th victory. To give this number some perspective,

David Pearson has the second most wins at 105.

Without doubt, part of the reason Petty was able to accumulate such a stunning number of victories was because back in NASCAR's early days, he would enter forty to sixty races a season. In 1967, the year he toted up those twenty-seven wins, he raced forty-eight times. Still, that's winning an astounding 56 percent of the time. And that is domination.

Richard Petty came by his talent honestly—his father was stock car pioneer Lee Petty, and, like his son, is one of NASCAR's 50 Greatest Drivers. Petty Sr.

Lee Petty, center, 50-year-old head of the most successful family in stock car racing, and his sons, Maurice, left, 25, and Richard, 26, look into an empty engine well of a new race car on July 15, 1964.

raced from 1949 to 1964, winning fifty-four races and grabbing the Series title three times. Richard started out in his dad's pit crew, given the title of "crew chief" at twelve. Lee wouldn't let his son drive until he reached NASCAR's legal driving age of twenty-one. But the day after that birthday, he drove in his first event, a dirt-track race in South Carolina, and finished sixth.

After posting DNFs in his next eight races, Richard finally earned his first checkered flag—or so he thought. While he proudly cruised to Victory Lane, another driver protested, complaining that the flag had dropped a lap too early. The irritated driver was judged to be right and the win was taken from Richard and given to the complainant...Lee Petty.

Just a year later, at the end of the 1959 season, twenty-two-year-old Richard was NASCAR's Rookie of the Year. Over the next thirty-five years, he would compile one of the most overwhelming records in stock car racing, while collecting seven National titles, en route to becoming the sport's most valuable and visible ambassador and earning his rightful title, the King.

Going into the Firecracker 400 on July 4, 1984,

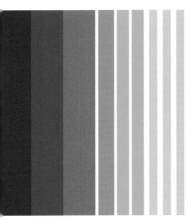

The fans had been expecting a battle royale and they weren't disappointed as the leaders, Petty and Cale Yarborough, pulled steadily away from the pack. With less than 4 laps to go, the 80,000 in attendance were on their feet, as Richard led Cale around the track at close to 200 mph.

King Richard had compiled an untouchable 199 victories. It was a perfect day to put the icing on the cake, with Ronald Reagan flying to Daytona, the first sitting president ever to attend a NASCAR race.

When the Independence Day event began, the president was in Air Force One just leaving Washington, D.C., but was still able to give the traditional "Gentlemen, start your engines" by radiotelephone. Later, at the track, the president even sat with race commentator Ned Jarrett and tried his hand at announcing.

The fans had been expecting a battle royale and they weren't disappointed as the leaders, Petty and Cale Yarborough, pulled steadily away from the pack. With less than four laps to go, the 80,000 in attendance were on their feet as Richard led Cale around the track at close to 200 mph. Suddenly, everything changed. Up ahead, the two leaders saw Doug Heveron's Chevrolet flipping into the air and knew instantly that a caution flag would quickly follow. With so few laps left, they also knew the race would almost certainly finish under caution—the first car to the yellow flag would win. With that, any long-term strategy they had went out the window; now it was pedal to the metal.

On the backstretch, Yarborough used his trademark slingshot maneuver to squeeze past Petty's number 43 STP Pontiac. But Richard fought back and managed to pull even with Cale's number 28 Chevy. As the cars careened around the last two turns, headed for the line, they bounced and banged each other. Petty thinks the last bump got him the 200th win. "The last bam squirted my car a little ahead," he said at the

Richard Petty takes the checkered flag to win the 26th annual Firecracker 400 stock car race in Daytona Beach, Florida. This was the 200th NASCAR win for Petty, beating out Cale Yarborough.

President Ronald Regan sits between Richard Petty and Bobby Allison during a lunch in the garage area prior to the Firecracker 400 at Daytona Speedway.

time. "We touched a couple of times coming for the line; enough to affect the cars but not enough to upset them. From where I sat, I knew I had him. I didn't know if it was a foot or a yard or three yards or an inch. I just knew I had him. At that point, the margin didn't make no difference."

Petty was first over the line, not more than a foot ahead of Yarborough. As the drivers had predicted, the race finished under caution and King Richard's historic victory was in the books. The crowd went crazy but no one was more ecstatic than Petty. "Probably the high-light of my whole career was winning the 200th race at Daytona on July Fourth in front of the president of the United States," he has said. "Winning 200 anywhere would have been great. Doing it under those circumstances and beating Cale, who I had been racing with for years, it was fantastic. Basically, it still is. I don't think there's anything to match that in the annals of racing."

Richard Petty's 200th win at the Firecracker 400 was the crowning glory of one of the most dominating careers in the history of sports. It's an unattainable record that forever enthrones him as the King of NASCAR.

Dale Earnhardt: The Man in Black

● ● ● ● ● ● ● ● ● ●

For the better part of a decade, from the mid-1980s to the mid-1990s, there was no one more dominant in stock car racing than Dale Earnhardt. He rose to become a sport-defining legend on the level of basketball's Michael Jordan or hockey's Wayne Gretzky. Earnhardt had a will to win that was nearly unstoppable, and the sight of his black number 3 Monte Carlo darkening the rearview mirror was enough to turn the strongest competitor's knees to jelly.

Dale, the only driver ever to win Rookie of the Year and the NASCAR Cup Series championship in consecutive years, once told a reporter, "Imagine you're leading the race on the last lap with me behind you. Would you want that? I would hate to have me behind me on the last lap." No wonder he was called the Intimidator.

One of the major keys to Earnhardt's success was that he always had his eyes on the prize. "I race to win," he explained. "Yeah, the money is part of it but I couldn't tell you what the purse is here....When you're a driver and you're racing, you want to win. That's about all."

Still, Dale's final Cup championship was not all about first-place finishes—it was just as much about consistency, the week-in, week-out battles that it takes to win the NASCAR points competition. In 1994, there were thirty-one races. Dale won just four of them, four less than Rusty Wallace, but he finished in the top five a mind-boggling twenty times. That's an amazing 64.5 percent of the time. In twenty-five of the races, he landed in the top ten—a career-high 80.6 percent record. That's the kind of domination that saps the will of the competition and makes an athlete seem more than mortal.

One of Earnhardt's most effective weapons was his incredible focus. "When I sit down in a race car it's like the first day I ever done it," he once said. "There's nothing else on my mind. I'm not sitting there while I'm racing pondering everything going on in my life. I'm focused on beating whoever is in front of me or behind me."

By Rockingham, the twenty-ninth race of that

Dale Earnhardt looks off into the distance in Riverside, California, at the Winston Western 500 on November 15, 1986.

1994 season, Dale was focused on the championship. He was 341 points ahead of Rusty Wallace, and with a good finish could clinch the Cup. Plus, there was something even more momentous at stake—Richard Petty's seemingly unreachable record of seven Cup championships.

Dale hadn't won a race for twenty weeks, since taking the checkered flag at Talladega in May. But on October 23, he locked up the Cup in style, edging Rick Mast at the line by 0.06 seconds to win his fourth race of the season. The victory and the Championship tied him with King Richard, and forever cemented Dale Earnhardt's reputation as one of NASCAR's greatest, and most dominant, drivers.

Jeff Gordon: The First of NASCAR's New Breed

• • • • • • • • • •

Although it's unlikely anyone there suspected it, "NASCAR: The Next Generation" began on November 15, 1992, at the season finale at Atlanta. As Alan Kulwicki clinched the Championship, forty-five-year-old Richard Petty was competing in the last race of his illustrious career, and twenty-one-year-old mostly unknown Jeff Gordon was driving in his first Cup series race.

"Jeff has been one of those people who changed what a race car driver is," said driver Jeff Burton on ESPN. "Look at Richard Petty. Look at Dale Earnhardt. Look at Cale Yarborough. Then look at Jeff Gordon. That's not the same picture. Jeff helped bring mainstream young America into our sport."

Gordon took care of the "unknown" part at warp speed. Just twelve months later, he was NASCAR's Rookie of the Year. Two years after that, in 1995, he won his first championship, ending Dale Earnhardt's quest for a record eighth championship. Jeff repeated in 1997, this time over Dale Jarrett, but his 1998 championship run was the season that made him a superstar. It was dominance on a Richard Petty level.

Gordon, who by 1998 had already been competing for over

Jeff Gordon in action during the NASCAR Napa 500 at the Atlanta Motor Speedway in Hampton, Georgia.

twenty years (he started as a six-year-old in quarter midgets), started out NASCAR's fiftieth anniversary season on a sour note. His motor dropped a cylinder at Daytona and he finished sixteenth. But the very next week, he came back and won Rockingham. There were a couple of races where he finished out of the top fifteen before Jeff, Hendrick Motorsports, and his pit crew got it together and picked up a second place at Darlington and a win at Bristol. That put him third in points. A disastrous outing at the Texas Motor Speedway dropped him to fifth, but the next week, at Martinsville, Gordon began a string of finishes that ranks him among NASCAR's greatest drivers.

A win at Lowe's Motor Speedway put Jeff in first place. An accident at Richmond dropped him back to third, but three weeks later a road course victory at Sears Point boosted him back into first—a position he would rule for the rest of the season. Beginning at Pocono and continuing through Indianapolis (where he picked up $1.64 million, the biggest payday in auto racing history), Watkins Glen, and Michigan, Gordon rolled up a record-tying run of four wins in a row. There were victories at New Hampshire and Darlington, five more top fives, then the checker at Daytona.

Even though Jeff locked up the championship at Rockingham, there was still something to shoot for: Richard Petty's modern-day record for wins in a season. Gordon answered that challenge at the Atlanta season finale by notching his thirteenth victory and tying the King's record.

Though Jeff has unfailingly attributed his enormous success to having one of motor racing's all-time best pit crews, his former crew chief Ray Evernham says they also had the best driver. "I look back and see what Jeff and I had," he insists. "And there is no doubt he was the greatest race driver I could have possibly had. In my mind, he is still the greatest race driver."

David Pearson: The Silver Fox
• • • • • • • • •

Unlike the proverbial tortoise-and-the-hare competition, slow and steady does not always win a NASCAR race. But, as any David Pearson fan can tell you, *fast* and steady can win you a *lot* of races. What David Pearson lacked in flash, he more than made up for with consistency and cunning. His smooth, stealthy moves on the track and the prematurely gray hair on his head earned him the nickname "the Silver Fox." And his rivalry with Richard Petty is one of the true legends of motor sports.

The Pearson-Petty duels were great for both the fans and NASCAR and a prime factor for the sport's increasing popularity during the 1960s and 1970s. Whenever it was Pearson versus Petty, a great show was guaranteed. These were not slam-bangers like Cale Yarborough and Bobby Allison, these were finesse guys. So fans were more likely to see a fight all the way to the finish line, not a crash on Lap 42.

Veteran driver and analyst Ned Jarrett says what made the pair so effective was their understanding of the machinery. "They knew how hard you could drive the car and expect it to be there at the end of the race." But that's not to say that the two wouldn't trade paint with a win on the line.

David Pearson's smooth and steady style made him NASCAR's dominant driver during the 1968 and 1969

David Pearson waits for his turn to qualify for the 1967 Daytona 500.

seasons. He had a combined record of twenty-seven wins, seventy-eight top fives, and eighty-two top ten finishes in those two seasons, interrupting King Richard's reign, earning him the championship two years running and his place as one of NASCAR's 50 Greatest Drivers.

While Pearson is second to Petty in wins, David actually has a better winning percentage. He won 105 out of 574 races, or 18.3 percent. Petty finished his career with 200 wins out of 1,185 starts for 16.9 percent. If Pearson had run as many races as Petty, there might have been a challenger to the King's throne.

Cale Yarborough: The Timmonsville Flash

• • • • • • • • •

Some people take several decades to discover their true calling in life. William Caleb "Cale" Yarborough found his at age eleven. That's when the kid from nearby Timmonsville, South Carolina, snuck under the fence at Darlington Raceway and watched the very first running of the Southern 500. That was 1950. Seven years later, when he was still seventeen, Cale drove in his first Southern 500 there.

Cale Yarborough raced through four decades—the 1950s into the 1980s. In that time, the drivers went from backroads bootleggers to rock 'n' roll style superstars. Cale earned his eighty-three victories (fifth on the all-time list) in every one of those four decades, but the 1970s were truly the "Yarborough Years" when Cale and his Junior Johnson–prepared race cars were true dominators.

One of the most aggressive drivers in NASCAR history, the "Timmonsville Flash" wasn't happy unless he was leading a race and pulling away. In fact, one of his most astonishing perform-ances came at Bristol on March 7, 1973. That day, Yarborough led every single lap of the Southeastern 500. By Lap 100, he'd lapped the entire field. But even with that commanding lead, Cale would not let up. He pulled into Victory Lane with a two-lap lead over second-place Richard Petty and a five-lap lead over third place Bobby Allison.

One of NASCAR's seminal moments came after some typical Yarborough aggressiveness. It happened at the Daytona 500 on February 18, 1979. Cale, who once said, "Drivin' a race car is like dancin' with a chainsaw!" tried to dance under Donnie Allison. Donnie dropped down to block him and the resulting crash took them both out. When the wrecked racers smoked to a stop, Yarborough and Donnie's brother Bobby jumped out and proceeded to wail on one another. That incredible, slam-bang finish, and, no doubt, the brawl that followed, helped implant NASCAR deep into the American consciousness.

Junior Johnson has a simple explanation for their incredible run in the 1970s—"Cale Yarborough is the best driver the sport has ever seen," he's said. "When you strap Cale into the car, it's like adding 20 horsepower."

Cale's most amazing achievement was capped off at Rockingham, the twenty-eighth race of the 1978 season. By winning his tenth race there, he clinched a third consecutive NASCAR Cup Series championship—a feat that had never been done before, and hasn't been done since. While setting that record, Yarborough won twenty-eight out of ninety races. That is domination.

Darrell Waltrip: A Force to Be Reckoned With

● ● ● ● ● ● ● ● ● ●

Long before Darrell Waltrip scored gigs as a race commentator and TV pitchman, he ran his mouth for free. The only price paid was the patience of those within earshot. Climbing the NASCAR ladder, DW was so outspoken that Cale Yarborough nicknamed him "Jaws." Though dismissed early on as a blowhard, in 1981 Waltrip proved his detractors wrong, demonstrating conclusively that his bite was even more fearsome than his bark.

The 1981 season didn't start out that way. Even though Darrell won four of the first fourteen races in his number 11 Mountain Dew Regal, engine failure in four of those outings cost him serious points. By race fifteen of the thirty-one-race season, Waltrip was a whopping 341 points back of Bobby Allison. What followed was the biggest championship comeback in the history of NASCAR, and a show of driving dominance that has rarely been equaled.

Darrell started his historic run at Riverside Raceway—winning that race and beginning a phenomenal string of finishes. Darrell completed every single one of the sixteen remaining races in the top ten, and placed in the top three in nine of them. In race twenty-five, at Dover Downs, Waltrip finally drove past Allison for first place—pulling ahead by a scant two points. But then Darrell totally dominated, winning the next four races in a row, bringing his checkered-flag total for the year

to a career-high twelve, and giving himself some breathing room.

Even after Waltrip's incredible run, Bobby Allison still had a mathematical chance to steal the championship from Waltrip in the season closer back at Riverside. And he tried mightily to do it. Allison won the race, but DW came in sixth, a high enough finish to secure the Cup championship by 53 points and earn him the distinction of achieving NASCAR's biggest comeback.

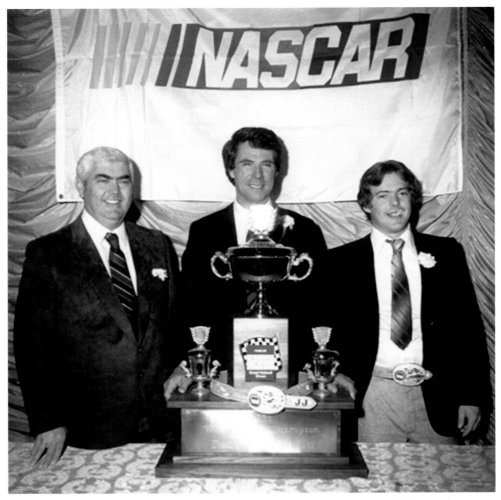

Darrell Waltrip driver, Junior Johnson car owner (left), and Tim Brewer crew chief (right), pose at the Winston Banquet in New York City honoring the 1981 Champions.

The 1981 championship was the first of three for Darrell Waltrip, during a twenty-nine-year career in which he piled up a staggering 96,550 Cup points. At the time of writing, that's the highest points total of any driver since the current NASCAR scoring system was installed in 1975.

All that time in the sport gives Darrell a great perspective—and a great appreciation—of the enormous strides NASCAR has made over the last three decades, both for him and the sport of stock car racing. "I have accomplished things beyond my wildest dreams," he has said. "They made us superstars. We weren't just race car drivers anymore. We weren't rednecks anymore. We were bona fide superstars, and more so today than ever before." And nowadays, when "Jaws" speaks, people really listen.

Rusty Wallace: One of the All-Time Greats

• • • • • • • • •

NASCAR's system of scoring championship points is complicated, and, some would argue, not completely fair. For example, missing a single race out of the season can cost a driver enough points to take him out of the Cup championship. Some have proposed a much simpler system—like having the driver with the most first-place finishes win the title.

It will almost certainly never happen, but if it did, it would make Russell William "Rusty" Wallace a very happy man. Rusty has one NASCAR championship in his trophy case; the 1989 Cup. But with that simpler system, he'd have three. That's because back in 1993 and 1994 Rusty Wallace and his Buddy Parrot–led team practically

Rusty Wallace acknowledges the crowd after winning the Spitfire Spark Plug 500 at Dover Downs International Speedway, Sunday, September 19, 1993.

ruled NASCAR. Dale Earnhardt Sr. may have been the Intimidator, but for two years Rusty was the Dominator.

Both Wallace and Earnhardt started the 1993 season on a mission launched at the NASCAR awards banquet the year before. That night the Cup was presented to Alan Kulwicki and it really stuck in their craws. "I'll never forget in '92 when Earnhardt and I were sitting in the back room," Rusty remembers. "He was twelfth and I was thirteenth [in the standings]. They started the banquet and he left. The very next year, we were so upset that I came out and won ten races and he won six."

Though Earnhardt ended up with the trophy,

Wallace outran him by a big margin. He won a career-high ten races, finished in the top five nineteen times, and led the most laps (2,860 out of 10,004). Wallace dominated early in the season, winning four of the first eight races. But over the next four weeks, an accident and mechanical misfortunes seriously crimped his championship chances. Despite slipping behind Earnhardt nearly 300 points, Wallace put on an amazing late-season charge.

With six races to go, Rusty was 181 points behind. A second at Martinsville combined with a bad finish by Earnhardt cut the lead to 82 points. Wallace won the next race at Rockingham and cut into the lead some more. But then, at Phoenix, Wallace was leading Earnhardt when his right front tire blew. Rusty ended up nineteenth, 126 points down, but he *still* wouldn't quit. He battled hard at Atlanta and won the last race of the year. Earnhardt finished tenth, a lap down, but collected enough points to finish 80 up on Wallace and win his sixth championship.

In 1994, Rusty once again had the most victories—eight to Dale's four—and led the most laps, only to have an accident at the spring Talladega, and a blown piston at summer Talladega, cripple his points drive. It added up to another dominating season for Wallace, but another Cup for Earnhardt.

Ned Jarrett: Gentleman Ned

● ● ● ● ● ● ● ● ●

You might say that Ned Jarrett's future was set in 1941, the year his dad let him drive the family car to church in little Newton, North Carolina. Even at nine years old, Ned took to it like a duck to water. It follows that his father really shouldn't have been surprised when his son turned down a career in the family lumber business to go race stock cars.

By 1960, twenty-three-year old Ned was winning Grand National races in a secondhand Ford he'd bought (on credit) from Junior Johnson for $2,000. Legend has it that he won just enough money that

season to pay Junior off. However, the very next year he won the championship, finishing in the top five in twenty-two out of the forty-six races.

In 1965, the man nicknamed "Gentleman Ned" for his calm demeanor and polite nature had one of the most dominant seasons in NASCAR history, with an amazing string of victories and top finishes. Of the fifty-four Grand National races he started that year, Jarrett won thirteen and piled up an incredible forty-two top five finishes.

Of all those races, and indeed, in all of Ned's career, no win was more impressive than the annual Labor Day

joust at Darlington. As usual, it was a steaming hot day. So hot that many of Jarrett's competitors were knocked out by overheating, blown engines and other heat-related mechanical problems. (Cale Yarborough was out after sailing over the guardrail and into the parking lot.) Ford had tried to help by supplying their racers with oversize aluminum radiators. But there was a problem—Darlington's asphalt shredded tires and the loose rubber clogged the radiators.

With 100 miles to go, Ned had built up an unprecedented fourteen-lap lead. But then he too started to overheat. His crew wanted him to pit and clean out the radiator. He certainly had enough of a lead. But Jarrett came up with a solution of his own.

"When I went into the turn, instead of backing off the accelerator," he recalls, "I cut the switch off to let the raw gas run in there so it would have a cooling effect, and, sure enough, it did....Every time I turned the switch back on and it cranked back up, the car would backfire. So the fans had a little action to cheer for because somebody sitting there with a fourteen-lap lead wasn't a very good race."

When Ned crossed the finish line, he had virtually sewn up the Grand National championship for 1965, and he had scored one of the fifty victories that make him the all-time winningest Ford Driver in NASCAR history. Jarrett may have repeated his amazing run the following year, but after he got off to a flying start, Ford suddenly pulled out its factory support of NASCAR. Ned did likewise, quitting the sport in his prime, at just thirty-four years old. Even so, his amazing fourteen-lap lead in the 1965 Southern 500 remains the largest margin by which anyone has ever won a NASCAR race.

Bobby Allison: Raging Rebel

● ● ● ● ● ● ● ● ● ●

Every time Bobby Allison strapped into a race car, it was his intention to dominate the competition. One of the most aggressive drivers in motor racing, Allison always drove at 10/10ths, pushing his equipment, his opponents, and himself to the ragged edge. That's how, in an injury-shortened twenty-five-year career, he was able to amass 336 top five finishes, and win the Daytona 500 three times—the last time at age fifty.

Bobby was a founding member of the legendary "Alabama Gang," made up of him, his brother Donnie,

fellow drivers Red Farmer and Neil Bonnett, and eventually Bobby's son Davey. Based in their adopted home of Hueytown, Alabama, they terrorized regional tracks around the Southeast, and then graduated to the NASCAR circuit.

Though Allison won his sole championship in 1983, it was his monumental battles with Richard Petty, Cale Yarborough, and David Pearson that make him one of NASCAR's dominators. Those fierce rivalries evolved into something more than racing; the ferocious nature of these competitors made beating each other something very personal.

In the early 1970s, slam-bang Allison-Petty duels were a fact of competition. So much so that each crew used to reinforce the cars' most vulnerable bodywork,

knowing the two were going to beat on each other. At one point, NASCAR even put out a publicity picture of the two arm-wrestling. Though Allison won more races in 1972 (ten to Petty's eight), Petty took the championship on points.

Their intense rivalry reached its peak that year at the North Wilkesboro Speedway as Bobby and the King battled to the finish line. For the final five laps of the race, the two walloped each other repeatedly, with Petty finally taking the checkers a couple of car

Bobby Allison's car begins to smoke during the last laps of his epic 1972 duel with Richard Petty.

The King clears a path.

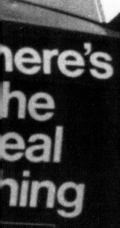

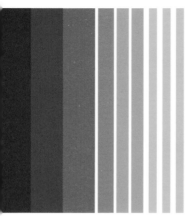

For the final five laps of the race, the two walloped each other repeatedly, with Petty finally taking the checkers a couple of car lengths ahead of Allison's battered and smoking racer.

lengths ahead of Allison's battered and smoking racer.

After the duel, both drivers were hopping mad. "He could have put me in the boondocks," seethed Richard. "He's playing with my life out there and I don't like it." Bobby shot back, "The other competitor had to wreck me to win, and that's what he did. I had so much smoke in my car I could hardly see." To put an exclamation point on Allison's statement, one of his enraged fans charged out of the stands and jumped Petty. A quick-thinking Maurice Petty clonked the attacker over the head with his brother Richard's helmet as the police moved in to take the rabid fan away.

Although there may not be a specific year that Bobby Allison "dominated" NASCAR, his illustrious career certainly earns him that distinction. He's one of the sport's 50 Greatest Drivers, and with eighty-four Cup victories, he's tied with Darrell Waltrip for third most wins of all time.

Tim Flock: The Highest-Flying Flock

● ● ● ● ● ● ● ● ●

Nowadays, often the most colorful aspect of NASCAR's drivers is their sponsor-patch-laden Nomex driving suits. Back in the old days, it was the drivers themselves who provided the color. Nobody is more representative of that early outlaw spirit than Julius Timothy Flock.

Tim grew up in the "Flying Flocks," nine brothers and sisters who were drawn to excitement. Family patriarch Carl Lee Flock, a former bicycle racer, died when Tim was just a year old, leaving the family to fend for themselves. To help out, oldest son Carl Jr. moved the family to Atlanta where he was bootlegging with their uncle, Peachtree Williams. Tim's older brothers Fonty and Bob delivered moonshine in cars they'd hopped up themselves, roaring down the backroads of Georgia outrunning the police and federal agents.

Around Atlanta and in many other southeastern cities and towns, the bootleggers would argue about who had the fastest car, and they'd settle the squabbles with impromptu races. At ten, Tim saw his first race, a go-round in a Georgia pasture where his brothers raced other local "whiskey trippers," knocking fenders and flinging mud. He was hooked. As Tim grew older, Fonty and Bob tried to get their youngest brother to "go straight" and finish school, but they couldn't keep him out of the driver's seat.

All three brothers (and sister Ethel) raced in the nascent racing league, but Tim was the highest-flying Flock, winning his first NASCAR championship in 1952. Three years later, in 1955, he hooked up with multimillionaire Carl Kiekhaefer, the inventor of the Mercury outboard motor, and their Chrysler 300s absolutely dominated stock car racing. Of the forty-five races held that year, Tim started on the pole in nineteen (still a NASCAR record), and he won eighteen (a record he held until Richard Petty broke it in 1967). Tim still has the highest percentage of races won (21.2 percent—40 victories in 189 starts) in Cup history, and that same year, 1952, he drove a 300SL Mercedes Gullwing Coupe to a win in NASCAR's first and only sports car race.

Despite Tim Flock's amazing driving record, he probably is more famous for his copilot during the 1953

Tim Flock, one of the most successful and colorful drivers in stock-car racing history, in 1960.

season—a rhesus monkey Tim named Jocko Flocko. Jocko had his own special seat and driver's uniform and rode beside Tim when he won a Grand National race at Hickory, North Carolina. Jocko's ride ended during his eighth race. Tim explained, "Back then the cars had a trapdoor that we could pull open with a chain to check our tire wear. Well, during the Raleigh 300, Jocko got loose from his seat and stuck his head through the trapdoor, and he went berserk! I had to come into the pits to put him out and ended up third. The pit stop cost me second place and a $600 difference in my paycheck. Jocko was retired immediately."

"THEY ACTUALLY WALKED AWAY?!"

"You certainly go into the race with the mindset of 'Let's miss the big wreck.' You have to think the big wreck is coming, and if you don't think the big wreck is coming, you haven't been watching racing very much."

2005 Talladega: The Biggest Big One

• • • • • • • • • •

There's a tale the locals tell around Talladega. They contend that the first speed-related fatality in the area was not a NASCAR, BGN, or IRL driver. It was a Talladega Indian chief who died during a horse race back in the 1700s.

Perhaps that's the reason Talladega, born in 1969 as Alabama International Motor Speedway, has always been regarded by some as a track that is haunted or

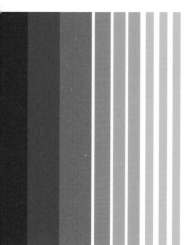

For today's Cup drivers, the most frightening thing about Talladega is the "Big One," a beast lurking in the shadows, poised to take out half the field in one metal-crunching, tire-screaming, smoke-choked megacrash.

jinxed or both. After all, this was the place where in 1973 Cup champion Bobby Isaac, in contention for the lead, suddenly pulled off the track and parked his race car. For the rest of his days, Isaac swore he did it because a ghostly voice had threatened him with death, and that if he had driven another lap, it would have been his last.

For today's Cup drivers, the most frightening thing about Talladega is the "Big One," a beast lurking in the shadows, poised to take out half the field in one metal-crunching, tire-screaming, smoke-choked megacrash. The Big One, the drivers say, is brought out by restrictor-plate racing. With more or less equal horsepower, no one car has a sizable advantage. So they inevitably end up in packs of twenty or more, running nose to tail, two or three abreast, inches apart at 190 mph.

Because Talladega is a points race, finishing is vital. Crashing can take a driver right out of the Cup championship competition. Driver Jeff Burton says that the primary objective at Talladega isn't necessarily winning—it's simply surviving. "You certainly go into the race with the mind-set of 'Let's miss the big wreck,'" he says. "You have to think the big wreck is coming, and if you don't think the big wreck is coming, you haven't been watching racing very much....You cannot finish forty-third in this race...and still win the championship."

To gain an advantage, drivers "bump draft," giving the car ahead a shove, which speeds up the front car and drags along the car that bumped it. All at three miles a minute. Veteran driver Geoff Bodine flat out doesn't like restrictor-plate racing at Talladega. "I think it's the most awful, dirtiest, nastiest, most dangerous racing in the whole wide world."

After 350 miles of the Aaron's 499 and four brief cautions, it looked like the Spring 2005 edition of Talladega might be Big One–free. But then, on Lap 133, the Big One bit. Hard.

Although accounts vary, it's widely believed that Dale Earnhardt Jr., in the number 8 Budweiser Monte

(*Overleaf*): **Talladega superspeedway rescue personnel look at the remains of some 22 cars that were involved in a wreck at Turn 1 during the Aaron's 499 race in Talladega, Alabama, Sunday, May 1, 2005. There was so much debris on the track officials red flagged the race for 45 minutes.**

(*Right*): **NASCAR drivers Kevin Harvick (29) and Jeff Gordon (24) lead a pack of cars at the start of the race.**

Carlo, was bump-drafting Mike Wallace's number 4 trying to get past Jimmie Johnson in the number 48, who was running inside Wallace. Johnson wasn't about to let Wallace get by and drifted up to block him. With nowhere to go, Wallace ran into Johnson, smashed into the wall, and then all hell broke loose.

The three Chevys careened off one another, setting off a spectacular chain reaction of spinning, banging cars and smoking, shrieking tires. Before the cloud of burnt

Some 22 cars were involved in the incident at Talladega Superspeedway, May 1, 2005. The race was won by Jeff Gordon.

Come True At

Aaron's 499
AT TALLADEGA

NASCAR driver Jeff Gordon celebrates after winning the Aaron's 499 race.

rubber cleared, twenty-eight of the cars were caught up, the biggest crash in NASCAR history.

Who was responsible? Dale Earnhardt Jr. blamed Jimmie Johnson, calling him an over-aggressive "idiot." Johnson claimed it was all in a day's racing. "I think if you look at the overhead shot of it," he insisted, "and you look at what the dynamics were of that, it's easy to see it. It's just guys racing two inches apart at 200 miles an hour. I mean, two inches isn't much. Once that's gone, you have a big wreck."

Ten of the drivers went to the infirmary in the Talladega infield, and, amazingly, none were seriously injured. After a forty-three-minute delay to clean up the track and repair the safety barriers, the race resumed. Both Earnhardt and Johnson were able to rejoin the battle, but, unbelievably, the two were involved in another accident on Lap 187. After Jimmie lost control and hit the wall, he dropped down the track and ended up taking out both Dale Jr. and pole sitter Kevin Harvick.

The eventual race winner was Jeff Gordon, who'd started beside Harvick in the front row. Having won Talladega before, Gordon knew that starting at number two was just fine. In fact, starting on the pole could be part of the Talladega jinx—since 1985, only one pole sitter has won the race.

After the victory, Jeff attributed his success to staying out in front of the Big One, and to the knowledge he'd gained racing at Talladega over the years. "This is the type of racing where experience is really key," Gordon said. "The more that I get used to watching my mirror, using the air, and having the kind of car I had today, I feel like I get better at restrictor-plate racing."

As for the bump-drafting that caused the 2005 Big One, Cup contender Tony Stewart had a simple suggestion. "If they want us to stop bump-drafting, take the [restrictor] plates off."

With the prospect of NASCAR taking the speed-robbing plates off practically nil, Talladega will remain one of the most exciting, and dangerous, races in the Cup Series, a haunted track where the Big One waits, looking to turn millions of dollars of machinery into steaming, smoking scrap metal.

1990 Bristol: Mikey's Miracle

• • • • • • • • • •

While Michael Waltrip's 1990 spectacular car-shredding wallbanger at Bristol Motor Speedway wasn't the biggest wreck in NASCAR history, it was certainly one of the scariest and most violent. Both the fans and Michael's big brother Darrell, watching from the pits, couldn't help thinking, "It'll be a miracle if he walks away from that!"

Normally, this wouldn't have been much more than a typical Busch Series fender bender. Even as it was happening Waltrip was unworried. "We reached Lap 171 of the 250 laps in the race," he said. "On the way to the front...I got on the outside of [Robert] Pressley.

He didn't have a ton of experience, and...he moved over and hit my left front tire with his car and it shot me right into that wall....When it hit, my mind was thinking, 'This won't be any real big deal.' "

What Michael didn't see was a section of the retaining wall sticking out. It was just past an iron gate recessed into the wall that was used to allow ambulances to enter the track and infield traffic to exit. As Waltrip's passenger-side door hit the end of the concrete wall, the wall latched on to the car. In a few horrendous seconds, the number 30 Kool-Aid Pontiac practically exploded. It looked like it was made of tin foil and tissue paper as it

disintegrated. The sheet metal peeling off, the roll cage tearing apart, the automotive debris pinwheeling in every direction, Michael slid down into the infield with nothing more to protect him than his driver's seat and a section of the roll cage.

After blacking out for a few seconds, he came to surrounded by extremely anxious people, including Darrell, who'd peeled what remained of the roof off his baby brother. For a moment, Michael didn't comprehend the commotion. "I remember as plain as day sitting there and a bunch of people messing with me....I didn't understand why they were so tore up about the wreck. Later, I found out the biggest part of the car left intact was the seat I was sitting in. Where the motor was supposed to be, I saw I could slide right out. I slipped out the front and stood right up." And, in fact, he raced the very next day.

How did Michael survive that horrifying crash? Certainly while he has NASCAR to thank for their stringent safety requirements, Waltrip believes it was a miracle. "There is no car built to withstand the crash that this thing had," he insists. "There is no other way to answer how I could be fine, unless God was with me and His angels just didn't allow me to get hurt. I reaffirmed my faith in Jesus after that."

Looking at the crash, it'd be hard to argue with Michael Waltrip's point of view. It is hard to figure out how anyone could walk away from a wreck as horrifying as his was without some kind of divine intervention.

Talladega 2003: Sadler's Flip-Flopping Ford
• • • • • • • • •

For over fifty years, one of the most appealing features of M&M's has been their "hard candy shell." Well, some of that hard coating must have been applied to Elliott Sadler's number 38 M&M's Ford, because on September 29, 2003, Sadler walked away from one of NASCAR's nastiest-looking wrecks.

The EA Sports 500 couldn't have started better for Elliott. The second-generation racer from Emporia, Virginia, qualified on the pole at nearly 190 mph, ran in the top ten for 151 laps, and even led for 23 of them. But he wouldn't make it to the finish line.

On Lap 181 of the 188-lap race, Sadler was in third place holding his line in the middle of the track when Dale Earnhardt Jr. got a message on his radio. "I was on the outside line and they said protect the middle," Dale recalls. "I turned down, I looked in the mirror and saw Elliott, and I turned back up. I think I might have spooked him into thinking I'm coming all the way down the middle lane."

The car of Elliott Sadler (38) flies through the air down the backstretch of the Talladega Superspeedway in Talladega, Alabama, Sunday, September 28, 2003. Sadler was flown to a local hospital for observation.

It turns out Elliott *was* spooked by Earnhardt's maneuver. "I was coming down the back straightaway in the middle....We had such a good run that I felt we could take the lead. I was looking at which line [race leader Michael Waltrip] was in, and all of a sudden, Junior just makes a hard left and I have to react to it, and then I cut across Kurt Busch's bumper."

That was the end of the race for Elliott and the beginning of a horrifying accident. When he was forced in front of Busch, Kurt's number 97 Ford smashed into his left side and his car started flipping. Sadler remembers, "When it hit me I was like, 'Oh my God,' and then, 'What's going to happen?' And then all of a sudden it just gets real quiet and I'm looking at the dirt and the asphalt. The whole pirouette, or whatever I did, seemed in slow motion the whole time."

As the horrified crowd watched, Sadler's car flipped violently end over end several times in the infield, finally coming to rest on its wheels. Miraculously, there was no Big One—all the other cars managed to avoid the flip-flopping Ford. Perhaps equally amazing was that, unlike a lot of previous crashes, the car did not spew sheet metal and tires all over the track. Crew members credited NASCAR's new tethering system, which ties the tires, hood, and trunk lid to the chassis.

As a testament to NASCAR's safety systems, two days after that horrible crash, Elliott Sadler was back in the driver's seat, testing replacement race cars in Kentucky.

Talladega 1998: Labonte Escapes a Big One to Take the Checkered Flag

● ● ● ● ● ● ● ● ●

There were 46 laps remaining in the 1998 DieHard 500 when an eerie, smoky silence drowned out the 34,000-horsepower roar at NASCAR's fastest and fiercest track. Talladega's 2.66 miles of high-banked asphalt had once again worked its black magic, and just three words of explanation were necessary: *the big one*.

Just a year earlier Mark Martin set an average speed record of 188.354 mph, completing a caution-free race at that same Alabama track in 2 hours, 39 minutes, and 18 seconds. Although the '98 edition had a couple of minor slowdowns—a yellow flag on Lap 109 for debris, and then again just 20 laps later to allow cleanup of oil from the blown engines of Johnny Benson and Kenny Irwin—another flat-out speed run to the finish was the story shaping up that day.

But with cars running inches apart at just a blink under 200 mph, it only takes a small wiggle in traffic to scramble the storyline.

The relative calm was shattered when Ward Burton tried to thread the needle near the front of the tightly bunched field. "I got my left front tires a few inches down on the apron and that got me loose," the soft-spoken Virginia driver admitted afterwards. "I got out of the throttle but the car went up the track and hit the three." That boot to Dale Earnhardt's left rear fender sent the black Monte Carlo zigzagging into Bill Elliott's Ford. Bobby Labonte, riding just ahead, watched in his rear-view mirror as things quickly went from bad to worse. "I saw the 94 car (Elliott) going the wrong way on the race track, and I knew it wasn't going to be good."

Earnhardt, up on two wheels, and an upside-down Elliott slammed together into the wall and slid backwards at close to 150 mph toward the first turn. As eighteen more cars piled up behind them, flames sprayed from Elliott's engine into Earnhardt's

Bill Elliott #94 McDonald's Ford crashes on lap 141 as Bobby Labonte #18 Interstate Batteries Pontiac takes the lead, followed by Dale Jarrett #88 Quality Care/Ford Credit and Jeff Gordon #24 DuPont Chevrolet during the Diehard 500 on April 26, 1998 at the Talladega Superspeedway in Talladega, Alabama. Labonte finished first.

driver's-side window. Elliott came away with a bruised sternum; Earnhardt, the last remaining Cup driver still wearing an open-face helmet, had second-degree burns to his face and neck. "It singed my hair and burned my mustache a little bit. I'll have to grow some new ones," Earnhardt told reporters after his post-crash medical checkup.

A red flag brought the Talladega track to a stand-still while crews cleared away the twisted wreckage. When the DieHard 500 went green nearly 30 minutes later, Bobby Labonte pulled off a delicate pass on older brother Terry with two laps remaining to take a hard-earned checked flag, and then told the assembled Victory Lane media contingent, "To finish a restrictor-plate race is a bonus, and to win one is even more of a bonus."

Talladega 1993: Rusty Wallace's Flying Finish

● ● ● ● ● ● ● ● ●

For Rusty Wallace, 1993 was a year of extremes. On the one hand, he was a serious contender for the championship—he'd win ten races that year and finished in the top ten in twenty-one of the thirty-races. On the other hand, he suffered through the two worst crashes of his career—the most spectacular and the most serious.

Rusty started the year on a bum note. On Lap 169 of the opening race at Daytona, Derrike Cope and Michael Waltrip collided and together shoved

Wallace into the backstretch grass. Rusty's number 2 Miller Pontiac barrel-rolled twice, flipped end over end, then twisted in the air eighteen more times. It looked terrifying, and when it was over, the car was utterly destroyed. Amazingly, Wallace escaped with a few stitches for cuts on his chin. "The one in Daytona, I had like twenty flips end over end and it wasn't real bad," he remembered. "But the one at Talladega...just knocked my lights right out."

That Talladega race was eight weeks after

Daytona and Rusty had come back like a champ. He'd won four races, the last three consecutively. He was hell-bent on collecting every point he could, and when the race, delayed by a spring shower, came down to a two-lap dash, the competition was fearsome. It took the first lap of the restart to get the cars up to speed, and when the flag dropped it became a 190 mph demolition derby.

There was all kinds of bumping and banging, and when Mark Martin tried to pass him on the outside, Wallace put him into the wall. While they traded paint, Ernie Irvan and Dale Earnhardt were doing likewise and Irvan took the lead, forcing

Earnhardt to drop back. In the next half-lap, Wallace managed to rear-end Jimmy Spencer, then sideswipe Dale Jarrett. Then, as they charged down the frontstretch toward the finish line, Earnhardt tried to pass Wallace and Wallace slid down to block him. With nowhere to go, Earnhardt smashed into

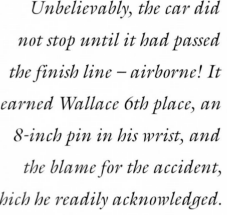

Unbelievably, the car did not stop until it had passed the finish line – airborne! It earned Wallace 6th place, an 8-inch pin in his wrist, and the blame for the accident, which he readily acknowledged.

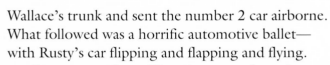

Wallace's trunk and sent the number 2 car airborne. What followed was a horrific automotive ballet—with Rusty's car flipping and flapping and flying.

Rusty remembers, "I went twenty-three times end over end and I woke up in a helicopter on the way to a hospital. I was pretty much alert through all the flipping. I just kept on saying to myself, 'When is the damned car gonna come to rest?'"

Unbelievably, the car did not stop until it had passed the finish line—airborne! It earned Wallace sixth place, an eight-inch pin in his wrist, and the blame for the accident, which he readily acknowledged. "When I moved over to block Dale, he was going four or five miles per hour faster than I was," he has said. "If it was anyone's fault, it was mine."

Rusty Wallace raced the next week, but blew up his transmission when the brace he had to wear got caught on the shifter. In all, he figures that bad move at Talladega cost him two or three hundred points. He lost the Cup chase in 1993 by eighty points—to, wouldn't you know it, Dale Earnhardt!

Daytona 1988: The King's Worst Crash

• • • • • • • • •

In stock car racing, crashes are equal-opportunity catastrophes—even the King of NASCAR wasn't immune to the forces of high-speed physics and bad fortune. In the late 1980s, race cars at the Daytona International Speedway were regularly breaking the 200 mph barrier. In 1987 Bill Elliott won the pole and set the all-time qualifying record at that track, with an unimaginable 210.364 mph. These were cars racing at

aircraft takeoff speeds, low-flying missiles with deadly disaster just a cut tire or steering bobble away.

So in 1988, NASCAR decided to slow the cars down and instituted restrictor-plate racing at Daytona and Talladega. Restrictor plates are simple aluminum plates with holes in them that mount beneath the carburetor and cut down the amount of air that gets to the engine. Less air, less horsepower. It works. To a point.

It did lower the speeds—in '88 the pole position at Daytona went to Ken Schrader at 193.823, almost 17 mph slower than Elliott the year before. Average race speeds dropped from the 170s to the 150s and lower. The problem is, at that speed, the drivers can run nose to tail, three abreast, just scant inches apart—a triple-track freight train where the tiniest mistake can mean derailment and instant tragedy.

That's how Richard Petty suffered what he considers the worst accident of his long career. Heading down the frontstretch on Lap 104, Petty was tapped in the rear by Phil Barkdoll's Ford and the number 43 STP Pontiac got sideways. Before Richard could collect it, Barkdoll tagged him again, hard.

With nowhere to go, A. J. Foyt smacked into Richard's front fender. Up went the rear end of the Petty car, which pirouetted on its nose before slamming back to the concrete on its roof. Then it bounced and barrel-rolled along the catch fence in front of the grandstands with sheet metal and parts flying every-where and fans ducking for cover. The car rolled four times, flipped, then came down right side up, only to be smashed into by Brett Bodine, spinning it four more times.

It was a truly horrifying sight, but Richard saw none of it. "I closed my eyes, held my breath, and

Richard Petty begins to flip in his Pontiac after coming into contact with Phil Barkdoll's Ford, shown right. The car flipped 7 times down the race-way during the Daytona 500 auto race on February 14, 1988. Petty reportedly was in good condition at a local hospital with a possible broken ankle.

then everything went black," he remembers. "I guess I blacked out....The next thing I remember was this guy stuck his head in the window and says, 'How you doing?' But I went blind. My eyes were open, but I couldn't see anything. I said, 'I'm all right, but I can't see anything.' He said, "Don't worry about it. It'll come back in three or four minutes.' "

Richard was rushed to the hospital, but unbelievably, before the race was over he was up and around, his eyesight and his love of racing nearly back to normal. He watched Bobby Allison win the 1988 Daytona 500 not from a hospital bed, but standing trackside.

Talladega 1987: Bobby Allison Flies Toward the Grandstands
● ● ● ● ● ● ● ● ●

Accidents are nothing out of the ordinary in NASCAR racing—they're as common as injury timeouts in football. But there are some accidents that have been so serious, so scary, that they have forced the France family to redefine the rules of racing. Bobby Allison's high-flying act during the May edition of the 1987 Talladega 500 was one of them.

Another reason had to do with pure speed. Bill Elliott set a now untouchable NASCAR qualifying-lap record of 212.809 miles per hour, and during that run he hit a top speed of over 230 mph, nearly four miles per minute!

With the whole field wailing around the track at over 200 mph, the fans were guaranteed an event to remember. They didn't have long to wait. On Lap 21, Bobby Allison's number 22 Miller Buick was flying down the frontstretch at around 205 mph when his engine blew. A piece of debris skipped under the car and punctured his left rear tire. The car slewed sideways, got backwards, then launched itself off the concrete heading for the grandstands.

Airborne at close to 200 mph, the car flew into the

twenty-foot-tall safety barrier, ripping a hundred feet of the steel fencing off its posts and spewing high-priced shrapnel onto the track and into the crowd before coming in for a hard landing. Another few inches higher and that 3,400-pound race car would have flown over the fence and into the stands where it almost certainly would have killed dozens and hurt hundreds. As it was, there were numerous injuries and one unfortunate race fan lost her eye.

Unbelievably, Bobby Allison was shaken up but not seriously hurt and was able to walk away from his demolished car. Since the cut tire turned the car backwards then airborne, he had been one of the few folks at Talladega who hadn't seen the accident. "It wasn't scary to me in the car," Allison said. "But I knew it was a bad wreck going on. I was really hoping that I wouldn't get hurt or hurt anybody else."

Allison's fence climb scared the Frances and their insurers. After reviewing the tapes, their provider insisted that NASCAR find a way to reduce the cars' speed to under 200 mph and protect the spectators or lose their coverage. Thus restrictor-plate racing was born, which did what it promised—it kept the speeds under 200. But it has also been one of the most hotly debated aspects of the sport ever since.

In spite of some drivers' objections to the horse-power-robbing plates, Bobby Allison prefers to err on the side of caution. "My opinion is that the restrictor plate is the best, most fair thing that NASCAR ever did," he said. "If we left the engines unrestricted, we'd have cars going 240 mph and they'd be landing forty rows into the grandstands."

Daytona 1984: Ricky Rudd's Crash at the Clash

• • • • • • • • •

In baseball, the title "Iron Man" belongs to Cal Ripken Jr., who played in an astonishing 2,632 consecutive games. It's a record that will likely never be broken. Likewise the incredible NASCAR Cup record of 752 consecutive starts. That unreachable streak belongs to NASCAR iron man Ricky Rudd. But at the 1984 Busch Clash at Daytona that streak very nearly came to an early and tragic end.

The problem seems to have been an almost imperceptible bump in Daytona's Turn 4. Both Cale Yarborough and Darrell Waltrip blamed it for wiping them out the year before—Cale in the middle of what would have been Daytona's first 200–plus mph qualifying run, and Darrell during the 500.

Ricky Rudd's accident happened during the 50-mile Busch Clash (now the Budweiser Shootout), the inaugural race of the season, held the week before the Daytona 500. Though not a points race, it is still a hotly contested event.

During the 1984 edition, Rudd was running in a string of cars when he suddenly lost control at that infamous spot in Turn 4. The car headed up the track, then appeared to kiss the wall before it swerved down the track. Out of control at nearly 190 mph, the number 15 Wrangler Ford beelined for the wall ringing the infield. Just before it smashed into the low concrete

barrier, air got under the car and, blessedly for Rudd, launched the racer airborne.

"All of a sudden it got real quiet," Ricky remembers. "I was glad it got airborne because it allowed me to hop over that wall, but then it came down the first time...and [I heard] the air go out of me. Like those game films in the NFL when a guy gets hit and all the air rushes out of his body. That 'ugh.' I heard that."

Rudd bounced and banged, his window net gone and his left arm flailing outside the window as the car twisted and turned seven times, throwing off sheet metal as it went. When the car finally came to rest, Rudd was a mess. His pupils were blood red, and he'd sustained torn cartilage in his rib cage, as well as body bruising. "I pretty much came loose inside the car [because] the seat broke in half. It wasn't much of a seat....That allowed me to have a lot of slack in the belts and I bounced around and got beat up pretty badly."

Unbelievably, Ricky, his face black and blue and swollen like a boxer's, was back in the driver's seat for the Daytona 500 the following week, keeping his streak alive. On race day, the swelling around his eyes was so bad, he had to duct-tape his eyes open to see! Rudd finished the race seventh, and won the next week at Richmond. That is an Iron Man.

Bristol 2002: Harmon's Close Call

• • • • • • • • •

On August 23, 2002, race fans in general, and one driver in particular, experienced a heavy dose of déjà vu. That day, Mike Harmon, during a Busch Series practice session at Bristol Motor Speedway, smashed into the same steel crossing gate Michael Waltrip had hit a dozen years earlier. The results were horrifyingly familiar—a race car ripped to ribbons, and a driver a miracle away from meeting his maker.

Harmon was the last person thinking about repeating Waltrip's spectacular stunt. "I told [Michael] I was sitting at home watching when it happened to him, and I couldn't believe what I'd seen," he said. "His car is down at Talladega, at the museum. To go by and look at it, you can't believe he lived through it. In a million years, I'd have never thought I'd get in a situation like that."

Actually, it may have been an even bigger miracle that Harmon survived his crash. Inexplicably, the six steel poles that reinforce the gate during racing were not in place. When Mike hit, the iron gate opened and directed his number 44 Chevrolet smack into the end of the concrete retaining wall, which proceeded to peel off the right side of his BGN racer like it was skinning a fish.

As it was happening, Mike remembers thinking it wouldn't be that serious. "I hit the wall and I thought it was going to be a normal deal," he said. "And suddenly I realized I was getting real close to the wall with my body."

To make matters even more deadly, the demolished car came off the wall and ground to a stop in the middle of the track. An instant later, the car was T-boned by Johnny Sauter. With a split second to react and Harmon sitting helpless right in front of him, Sauter literally had the other driver's life in his hands.

"I just tried not to hit the driver's door," Sauter remembers. "That was the main thing. I think I kind

of drove right through the car. It happened so fast....I'm just glad I didn't hit him or even kill him."

Mike Harmon made it through the accident with little more damage than body bruises, but the voices of the drivers were loud and angry. They demanded to know why the steel poles weren't in place and why that gate was still there since Bristol now had a tunnel to move people and vehicles in and out of the infield. The answer was "human error," an inexcusable mistake that cost one racing team a very expensive piece of machinery, and almost cost Mike Harmon his life.

Rescue workers ruch to the aid of BUSCH Series driver Mike Harmon, red helmet, after hitting the wall coming out of Turn 4 during practice for the Food City 250 at Bristol Motor Speedway Thursday, August 22, 2002, in Bristol, Tennesee.

Darlington 1965: Cale's Moon Shot

● ● ● ● ● ● ● ● ● ●

If all you looked at were Cale Yarborough's amazing career statistics, you'd understand why he is enshrined in the International Motorsports Hall of Fame, and why in 1998 he was named one of NASCAR's 50 Greatest Drivers. But that's not the whole story. Called by one sportswriter "a mixed package of physical skill, nerve and intellect," Cale was one of motor racing's toughest competitors, an

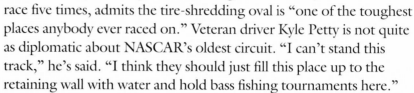

aggressive driver whose larger-than-life presence helped NASCAR establish itself as a legitimate sport.

One of the events that helped launch stock car racing and Cale Yarborough was coverage of the 1965 Southern 500 by *ABC's Wide World of Sports*. That day their television cameras captured one of the most spectacular crashes in NASCAR history, and for years they included the footage in their famous opening credits.

If there was anyone who knew Darlington, it was Yarborough. He grew up nearby and used to sneak into the track to watch the races. Still, competing on that track was one of his greatest challenges. Even Cale, who won the race five times, admits the tire-shredding oval is "one of the toughest places anybody ever raced on." Veteran driver Kyle Petty is not quite as diplomatic about NASCAR's oldest circuit. "I can't stand this track," he's said. "I think they should just fill this place up to the retaining wall with water and hold bass fishing tournaments here."

Back in 1965 the track didn't have retaining walls, just door-handle-high guardrails—the source of "Darlington Stripes"—a souvenir race cars got from scraping the metal barriers. Cale didn't get stripes that year, but he did get wings. His number 27 Banjo Matthews Ford was trailing race leader Sam McQuagg's number 24 Betty Lilly Ford. When Cale tried to force his way past, the two collided, sending McQuagg into the guardrail. Yarborough, however, sailed over the guardrail, which was set atop a forty-foot embankment.

Cale has a vivid memory of that moment. "When you get in trouble on a racetrack, it gets kind of quiet because your wheels are off the asphalt," he said. "I saw some grass as I was going over, and I knew there wasn't any grass on the track, so I knew it was going to be a hard hit."

Yarborough's prediction was accurate. With ABC's camera tracking him, his Galaxy flew into the grassy parking lot two stories below, flipped violently several times, and came to rest against a light pole. It looked like Yarborough's aggressive style might have finally cost him his life. To everyone's amazement, Cale walked away from the car with little more than a scratch under his eye.

Later, when interviewed by ABC's Chris Economaki, Yarborough joked about his unscheduled space flight. "The astronauts got nothing on me." That was just the kind of colorful comment that helped make Cale Yarborough one of the true legends of NASCAR.

Cale Yarborough sets sail over the second turn guard rail in the 1965 Southern 500 at Darlington Raceway. Giving him a push is Sam McQuagg.

Chapter Five
THE RECORD BREAKERS

At the season's end, Jeff Gordon was not chasing the Cup, he was in a high-octane race with history— in the last four weeks of the season Gordon drove his way right into the record books, parking there in the spot next to the King himself, Richard Petty.

Jeff Gordon's Season to Remember

• • • • • • • • • •

In racing, it's not how you start but how you finish that counts. Just compare the first four races of Jeff Gordon's 1998 season to the last four: he started the season by finishing a disappointing sixteenth at the Daytona 500 after dropping a cylinder, and after a win at Rockingham in the second week, he plunged again, to seventeenth and nineteenth in Las Vegas and Atlanta over the next two weeks, and he was just seventh in the standings.

Gordon had never in his career started off so badly. He'd won Rookie of the Year in 1993 with seven top

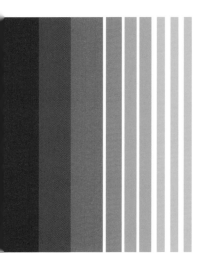

After a third-place finish in Michigan and a second-place in the Pocono 500, Gordon went on a historic run, one that nearly matched the best of Richard Petty and David Pearson in the 1960s and 1970s.

five finishes, then proved he could take the next step in 1994 with two wins and an eighth-place finish in the Cup standings; in 1995 he'd made the leap from budding star to superstar with seven wins and seventeen top five finishes, capturing his first crown; in 1996 he'd finished second on the season just thirty points behind the more consistent Terry Labonte despite outshining Labonte with ten wins and twenty-one top five placements. But Gordon came back with another stellar year in 1997, winning ten times and landing in the top five twenty-two times. In that year, he'd kicked off in high gear, winning both Daytona and Rockingham, then

finishing fourth at Richmond in the third week.

But the slow start proved irrelevant. At the season's end, Gordon was not chasing the Cup, he was in a high-octane race with history—in the last four weeks of the season he drove his way right into the record books, parking there in the spot next to the King himself, Richard Petty.

This was no gradual turnaround—Gordon would only finish out of the top ten twice more in the final twenty-nine races, and twenty-five of those twenty-seven strong endings would be in the top five. By his second win, six weeks into the season, he'd moved up to third place, and he'd briefly move into first in the Winston Cup race in late May. Still, it wasn't until midway through the season that it became apparent that this season would be a truly special one for Gordon.

After a third-place finish in Michigan and a second-place in the Pocono 500, Gordon went on a historic run, one that nearly matched the best of Richard Petty and David Pearson in the 1960s and 1970s. Beginning with a win at Sonoma in the Save Mart 350, Gordon reeled off seven wins in his next nine races. In the middle of that stretch he tied the modern record with four straight wins at the Pennsylvania 500, the Brickyard 400, the Bud at the Glen, and the Pepsi 400.

A "down" week by Gordon's standards left him in fifth at the Goody's 500, but he won the CMT 300 the

(*Overleaf*) Driver Jeff Gordon #24 leads Mark Martin #6 by a car's length going into the last lap during the Pepsi 400 at the Michigan Speedway in Brooklyn, Michigan. Gordon went on to win the event.

Jeff Gordon celebrates following the NASCAR Brickyard 400 at the Indianapolis Motor Speedway in Indianapolis, Indiana.

At age 27, Gordon is the youngest driver to win three Winston Cup championships. He's tied Richard Petty's modern record of 13 victories in a season, which had stood alone for more than two decades.

following week with a dynamite comeback to edge Mark Martin, who by then trailed him by just 67 points in the Cup standings. Jack Roush, who headed Martin's team, accused Rick Hendrick, DuPont, and number 24 of cheating. Gordon's team was cleared and then set the record straight in the very next race.

Gordon made history on Labor Day weekend—and earned a million-dollar bonus in the process—by capturing his fourth straight Southern 500. Although Jeff Burton led for 273 of the 367 laps, Gordon finished an impressive 3.631 seconds in front of him at Darlington. Suddenly, Gordon also had a 199-point lead over Martin for the Cup.

Still, if there was one knock remaining against Gordon it was that he had never been a strong season finisher: in 1995 he hadn't managed a win in the last six races and finished twentieth or below in three of those as Dale Earnhardt whittled his lead from 275 points down to 34 before time ran out on the season; in 1996 Gordon had led Labonte by 111 points with four races to go before losing by 30 thanks to two dismal runs in those final weeks; and in 1997 he hadn't won, or even finished in the top three, over his last seven races, as his 139-point lead nearly evaporated, leaving him a mere 14 points ahead of hard-charging Dale Jarrett. (It was the fourth-closest finish in history.)

So for Gordon to truly live up to his billing in 1998 he wanted to finish strong. After the Southern 500 he ran into a "slump" of sorts, failing to win in his next five tries. Still, he finished second in four of those and fifth once, expanding his lead over Martin to 288 points.

He had matched his career high with ten wins and had his third title wrapped up, but Gordon did not coast through the final month. He slammed on the accelerator and left every driver short of Petty in the dust.

At Daytona on October 17, Gordon picked up his first win in six weeks in the Pepsi 400, which had been postponed from its usual July Fourth date because of dangerous wildfires. It was the first time he had ever won a race in October. After a seventh-place finish the following week it seemed like any chance of tying Petty was gone since Gordon needed to win both of the remaining races and he'd *never* won a race in November.

Gordon, however, was unstoppable. At the ACDelco 400 at Rockingham, Dale Jarrett and Rusty Wallace dominated, leading for 347 of 393 laps between them, but Gordon came on strong to win by just a half-second over Jarrett, officially clinching the Cup crown.

The fates threw another obstacle in Gordon's way for the final race, the NAPA 500 in Atlanta. This was, of course, the site of one of his worst performances of the year back in March. This time around, rain played havoc with the race, turning it into a marathon yet also shortening the 325-lap race down to 221. But this one saw Gordon in command—he'd led for more than half the race when it was ended prematurely, so there was no doubt that he had truly and fully earned win number thirteen, which tied him with Petty for the most in the modern era.

Gordon had a total of twenty-six top five performances to win the Cup by 364 points, the third highest margin of victory over the previous two decades. In celebrating its fiftieth anniversary NASCAR had hoped for a memorable season. Jeff Gordon made it happen.

Handsome Harry's Amazing Streak
• • • • • • • • •

Harry Gant was an old man in a young man's game. It had always been that way—after all, he didn't make his Winston Cup debut until he was thirty-nine, and that was back in 1979. He didn't win his first NASCAR Cup series race until his 107th start, when he was forty-two. But in 1991, during his September to remember, Gant seemed to be fueling up at the fountain of youth.

He began what became known as "The Streak" on September 1, by winning the Heinz Southern 500 at Darlington Raceway. Every race Gant won set a new record for "the oldest driver ever to win."

"Handsome Harry" was busy—and productive the next weekend at Richmond International Raceway. He won the 200-lap Busch Grand National race on September 6, then going twice the distance in the Miller Genuine Draft 400 NASCAR Cup race the next day, prevailing even after he had to slam on the brakes and spin 360 degrees to avoid an out-of-control car. At Dover Downs six days later Gant again doubled down, winning a 200-lapper and the Peak Antifreeze 500. In just over two weeks he had won five races on three challenging tracks. On September 22 in the Goody's 500, Gant would try tying the modern record of four straight Cup wins—but unlike Cale Yarborough (1976), Darrell Waltrip (1981), and Dale Earnhardt (1987), he would be going for his sixth straight win in that span.

This race would be the toughest of all. All the attention paid to The Streak—which overshadowed Dale Earnhardt and Ricky Rudd's battle for the Cup Series—meant everyone would be gunning for Gant and they'd be doing it on the tightest of tracks, the little half-mile oval at Virginia's Martinsville Speedway.

Gant was dominating—out front for almost 200 laps—when his great run was nearly derailed. On the 376th lap, Rusty Wallace, overly eager to pass the leader, took Turn 3 way too hard for such a tight track. He started spinning and struck Gant's car, spinning him out, causing Derrike Cope to plow into him.

Harry Gant holds the winning trophy after the 1991 Goody's 500 at Martinsville Speedway.

Gant's crew did a superb job of getting him back on track, but the driver was so angry at Wallace's tactics—he believed Wallace had to know he couldn't make that turn and would hit him—that it took him nearly ten laps to calm down. (Wallace was unrepentant afterwards, though he apologized to Gant the next week.)

But he soon refocused. Having restarted in twelfth place with 120 laps to go, he climbed to fifth by the 425th lap, to third ten laps later, and back into first with more than fifty laps remaining. But Brett Bodine—who bumped Gant when he went by—was coming on strong too and briefly passed him on lap 449. Gant was having none of it. He pulled even, and then in the 453rd lap he regained the lead for good. He'd finish first by 1.1 seconds over Bodine. "Maybe they figured the only way anybody could beat me was to rough me up," Gant said afterwards before rubbing it in. "It makes 'em feel bad that I can pass 'em clean after they've hit me. It lets 'em know they're not as good as they think they are."

On September 29, Gant became the oldest person ever to start from the pole position and nearly win his fifth straight Cup race in the Tyson Holly Farms 400 at the North Wilkesboro Speedway, leading most of the way before brake troubles hit. With nine laps left, Earnhardt passed him, winning by 1.2 seconds to preserve his share of the record.

Still, it had been a remarkable month. From then on, Gant was no longer just "Handsome Harry" or "the old man." He was "Mr. September."

Bobby Isaac celebrates in victory lane after winning the 1969 Greenville/Pickens event.

Bobby Isaac's Twenty Poles in '69

• • • • • • • • •

Bobby Isaac was racing's ultimate outsider, but nothing could stop him from getting to the inside: despite being ostracized by his fellow NASCAR drivers in 1969, he claimed a single-season mark of twenty pole positions. (The season that year was fifty-four races, far longer than the modern circuit.)

Perhaps it shouldn't be surprising that he broke the record at the same time that other racers were shunning him; after all, he had spent a lifetime overcoming adversity and obstacles. Isaac was the second youngest of nine kids and lost both parents while still

young—his father died when he was six, his mother when he was sixteen. He dropped out of school at thirteen and spent much of his youth bouncing from one unsatisfying job to the next (working in a sawmill, then on an ice truck, in a pool hall, and a cotton mill). Even when he discovered racing, Isaac continued struggling—despite winning races against the likes of Ned Jarrett, David Pearson, and Ralph Earnhardt in 1958, he had a tough time gaining traction. Several times his career got shoved to the side of the road for an array of reasons—mechanical problems, crashes, disputes with his backers, and feuds between NASCAR, his backers, and car companies.

In 1966, Isaac hit a new low, as a man without a car or team. His career seemed finished. But the next year he hooked up with K&K Insurance and his life shifted into high gear. He finished fourteenth in points in 1967 but jumped to second in 1968, actually leading the chase for much of the year.

Finally he'd proven himself as a driver, but that didn't mean he was one of the boys. Even in the macho, be-your-own-man world of Southern racing, Isaac was considered independent...too much so, in fact. Fellow drivers like Richard Petty thought him aloof, and in 1969 when they formed the short-lived Professional Drivers Association to challenge some of NASCAR's practices only one top driver was left out: Bobby Isaac.

Isaac's feelings were hurt but he shrugged it off with his best performance to date. Although he finished just sixth in points (NASCAR based points on race distance and Isaac ran many short races), he won seventeen races, more than any driver that year, including his first superspeedway win in the Texas 500. He even won the National Motorsports Press Association's Most Popular Driver award, which must have been rewarding considering the drivers' union debacle. The following season, Isaac would produce his greatest success of all, winning the NASCAR Cup season with eleven more wins. But it was his twenty pole positions in 1969 that landed Isaac on the inside...of the NASCAR record book.

Bill Elliott: NASCAR's Fastest Driver

● ● ● ● ● ● ● ● ●

There was only one man who could drive faster than Bill Elliott and that was Elliott himself.

Elliott was always at the front of the pack pushing the boundaries at the intersection of speed and safety. When he took to the course in Talladega to qualify for the Winston 500 on April 30, 1987, no one had challenged the speed record of 212.229 mph he'd set in the qualifier on that very track the previous year.

And no one else would match that old mark. Bobby Allison's Buick LeSabre topped out at 211.797, and his son Davey Allison, who'd eventually win the race that Sunday, finished third on the Thursday qualifying round at 210.610.

But Elliott, a six-foot-one, 185-pounder from Dawsonville, Georgia, was not intimidated by his old mark. Supported by his father, George, Elliott and his brothers Ernie and Dan had pursued racing with unbridled ferocity. He'd entered his first NASCAR Cup race in 1976, earned his first pole position in 1981, and by the following year had the financial backing to race the entire circuit. He captured his first victory in 1983 and by 1985 was a speed demon to be reckoned with, racing to eleven pole positions and eleven victories that year, earning the nickname "Million-Dollar Bill" in reference to his prodigious winnings.

In his Ford Thunderbird, Elliott tore around the 2.66-mile high-banked oval in just 44.998 seconds. That averaged out to 212.809 mph and a new record.

The race that Sunday would ensure the endurance of Elliott's one-lap mark. With the drivers struggling to maintain control over their increasingly powerful machines, defending champion Bobby Allison endured one of the most terrifying crashes ever as his car lifted into the air, back end first, then smashed into a fence and sent parts into the stands where four people were injured. The race was delayed for two and a half hours.

In the aftermath of this accident NASCAR introduced carburetor restrictor plates.

Elliott would go on to make a career of setting speed records under various conditions and at assorted tracks, all while amassing forty-four victories and fifty-five pole positions, placing him in the all-time top twenty and top ten respectively. Equally impressive was that he remained an inherently good guy, winning the National Motorsports Press Association's Most Popular Driver award for a record sixteen straight years—stopping only when he felt compelled to take his name off the ballot so others might have a chance to win.

Bill Elliott in action at Talladega, 1987.

Richard Petty: The Babe Ruth of NASCAR

• • • • • • • • • •

In 1967, NASCAR needed a leader. It got a King. Richard Petty had emerged as a star in 1962, but just three years later he'd left NASCAR for drag racing over a feud between NASCAR and Chrysler (which made his car) about engine size. He returned in 1966, winning his second Daytona 500, but NASCAR was again plagued by similar problems with Ford's drivers.

By 1967, order had been restored, but questions lingered about NASCAR's future. With its image

damaged, with original stars like Lee Petty, Fireball Roberts, Ned Jarrett, and others done or nearly done, and with attendance falling, could the sport rebound and still command an audience? Even Richard Petty himself said, "If there is any glamour in the sport, I haven't found it."

But then Petty climbed in his blue-and-red number 43 and began his heralded march of triumphs.

In that season he won twenty-seven races, captivating race fans and bringing new ones into the stands. Sure, that record owes its existence to the fact that he raced forty-eight times that year but still, twenty-seven of forty-eight is a remarkable percentage. (He also had eleven other top five finishes.) Early in the season he broke his father Lee's NASCAR record of fifty-four career wins. But that would not even be the highlight of his season.

Petty's most remarkable accomplishment in 1967 was the one that had nothing to do with the length of the season: from August to October of that year, he won ten straight races.

By comparison, no driver in the post–1972 era has won even five straight—Petty and Bobby Allison each won five straight in 1971 and David Pearson won nine of ten that he entered in 1973, but he skipped numerous races in between. The hoopla these days when a driver wins four straight illuminates just how unimaginable winning ten straight is.

Petty won at Winston-Salem, Columbia, Savannah, Darlington, Hickory, Richmond, Beltsville, Hillsboro, Martinsville, and finally North Wilkesboro; he earned six pole positions along the way. Finally, at Charlotte Motor Speedway Petty fell and Buddy Baker won. The King had lost, but everyone in NASCAR was shouting, "Long live the King!"

He became national news. After the streak ended newspapers were noting that Petty had finished second in a race, not even bothering to mention the winner. And since his ability to charm the media equaled his ability to outrace rival drivers, he became the Babe Ruth of NASCAR, both for his larger-than-life statistics and for the way he helped revive the sport. With his cowboy hat and sunglass, Petty was definitely his own man with his own image. He became, quite simply, as his new nickname pronounced, the King.

Richard Petty in his blue and red #43, battling door to door during his amazing winning streak in 1967.

Andretti/Foyt: Daytona and Indy Champions
• • • • • • • • • •

Mario Andretti and A. J. Foyt stopped speaking to each other decades ago for a variety of reasons, but they've always had plenty in common: they're two of the greatest drivers of all time, in terms of longevity and dominance. Yet when their names come up it's rarely about stock cars. So what are they doing in a

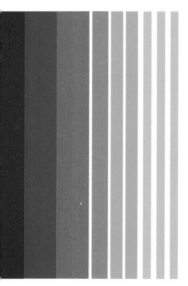

Mario Andretti and A. J. Foyt stopped speaking to each other decades ago for a variety of reasons but they've always had plenty in common: they're two of the greatest drivers of all time, in terms of longevity and dominance.

chapter on NASCAR record breakers?

Well, that's another thing they have in common—they were also among the most versatile drivers of all time, succeeding behind the wheel of virtually every type of race car imaginable. And that's why they are the only two drivers in history to win both of America's two most famous races, the Indy 500 and the Daytona 500.

Andretti is the more unlikely of the two to have

Mario Andretti tries out the bubbly in Victory Lane after winning the 1967 Daytona 500.

A. J. Foyt holds a flag and is kissed by two 76 girls after winning the Daytona 500 at the Daytona Speedway on February 14, 1971 in Daytona Beach, Florida.

pulled off the feat, yet he did it first. He gained his first Indy championship in 1966 and would win it three more times through the years. But he only won one Indianapolis 500, in 1969, his second championship year. That was actually two years after his crowning NASCAR moment in 1967 when he won the Daytona 500.

Although it may be surprising that Andretti won only one Indy 500, it's more surprising that he won the Daytona race—that was at the start of a year in which one driver, Richard Petty, would rule NASCAR in an unprecedented manner, winning twenty-seven races. He had already won the season opener. Andretti, by contrast, would never again taste success in NASCAR Cup racing. He had raced in only four NASCAR events before that year and competed only fourteen times all told—in fact, outside of that huge win he'd never again finish in the top five.

Still, no one could deny his golden moment. While most of the biggest names were plagued by engine, clutch, and oil problems—Petty (eighth place), Bobby Isaac (nineteenth), David Pearson (twenty-fourth), Cale Yarborough (thirty-ninth), and Bobby Allison (fortieth)—Andretti led for 112 of the 200 laps enroute to victory.

Foyt finished just thirty-seventh that year, but 1967 would also mark his third year winning the Indy 500. And he'd shown he wasn't just a NASCAR dilettante— he'd already won two NASCAR races and had three other top fives. In fact, Foyt would post respectable overall Cup-level numbers, driving 128 races in his career and pulling in twenty-nine top fives, which included seven wins. His peak would be 1971 and 1972, when he drove thirteen races, won four, and had nine total top five finishes. His second-to-last of those wins would be at Daytona. On a day when Petty, Yarborough, and the other elite drivers struggled again with car problems, Foyt led for a whopping 167 laps and took the checkered flag a full lap ahead of second-place finisher Charlie Glotzbach.

Both men would go on to other big wins on other tracks—Andretti in Formula One, Foyt at Le Mans—but it would be their unique achievement at America's two premier races that would land them in the record book together, forever.

Dale Jr. Tames Talladega

• • • • • • • • •

Racing at Talladega—with its restrictor plates, emphasis on aerodynamics, and penchant for big wrecks—is supposed to be one of Cup racing's most formidable tasks. But in 2001 and 2002 Dale Earnhardt Jr. made it look easy, winning three straight times on the 2.66-mile track to tie the record Buddy Baker set back in 1976.

It was only when Junior tried breaking the record, in the April 2003 Aaron's 499, that he experienced the full depth of the challenges of winning at this Alabama superspeedway.

Earnhardt's day got off to a rocky start, which almost meant no start at all. First, several members of his crew forgot to change their clocks for daylight savings time and arrived an hour late. Then they discovered water in the oil tank and, worried about a leak, rushed through a last-minute engine change. As a result, Earnhardt, who'd qualified thirteenth, started his familiar number 8 Budweiser Chevrolet dead last among the forty-three cars.

Not a good beginning for a driver who'd begun the season in a rough patch, finishing just thirty-sixth in the Daytona 500, thirty-third in Rockingham, and sixteenth in Bristol—even his two second-place finishes felt frustrating because Earnhardt had thought he would win those drives.

For the first half of the race, Earnhardt felt his car was compromised, especially because there was plenty of gouging going on amongst the highly competitive front-runners—this race featured forty-three lead changes among sixteen drivers. "I don't think I've ever torn up a car like we did today at a [restrictor] plate track," he said afterwards. "You had to really be tough or get knocked the hell out of the way."

But it was about to get a lot messier. On just the fourth lap there was a doozy of a crash when Ryan Newman's front tire blew and Mark Martin slammed

Dale Earnhardt Jr. in the #8 Budweiser Chevrolet passes Matt Kenseth
in the #17 Dewalt Ford for the lead during the NASCAR Winston Cup Aaron's 499
on April 6, 2003 at Talladega Superspeedway in Talladega, Alabama.

into him—all told twenty-seven cars were caught up in the wreck. Earnhardt did a fine job of navigating his red Monte Carlo through the wreckage, but took enough of a hit to the car's nose from debris that he required a whopping eleven pit stops in the first twenty laps.

There was little doubt that Earnhardt was one of the tough ones. This was his chance to prove he could win not only as a front-runner but in come-from-behind fashion. It never got any easier for him and by the end Earnhardt was ensnared in a major controversy, but he had his record.

With three and a half laps remaining, Earnhardt made his move to the front, driving inside the dueling leaders Jimmie Johnson and Matt Kenseth on the backstretch. On the path, Earnhardt's tires went below the yellow line on the track's inside edge, which is against the rules in restrictor-plate races. When Earnhardt was not penalized, the other drivers howled long and loud in protest, with some claiming NASCAR favored the son of racing's favorite son. But NASCAR officials, who would not show the footage to the media, claimed Earnhardt was already past his two rivals when his left side tires touched the yellow line.

On the track, Earnhardt and Kenseth drove neck and neck for another lap before Earnhardt caught a big aerodynamic draft from Kevin Harvick and pulled away. After a grueling afternoon, Junior had the eighth win of his career and a record fourth straight at Talladega.

David Pearson at the Pole

● ● ● ● ● ● ● ● ● ●

David Pearson could never quite keep up reputation-wise with his main rival Richard Petty. The King overshadowed him, but Pearson, who often ran only the big-money races, not the whole season, still racked up an impressive list of accomplishments, including three Cup championships, the second most all-time wins with 105, and 113 poles. But there was one arena in which Pearson undeniably outshone Petty.

When it came to qualifying at the Charlotte Motor Speedway, Pearson was in a class by himself, piling up fourteen poles including an amazing eleven straight during a five-year span from October 1973 through October 1978.

Pearson's career began in 1960 but really took off in 1968 when he posted twenty-seven wins and thirty second-places in a two-year span. But he was no flash in the pan, winning forty-three races from 1973 through 1978. Driving the Wood Brothers number 21 Ford in that era, Pearson was primed for the kind of speed it took to grab the pole at Charlotte's 1.5-mile superspeedway.

"The Wood Brothers had the car set up on the edge," he once said, explaining that they used many little tricks like adding special grease to the wheel bearings. "If something had happened and I had to hit the brakes, I wouldn't have had any. They were pushing everything to the limit."

With Pearson making the pole his personal possession, fans started skipping the qualifiers since they knew the outcome. That rattled track president Humpy Wheeler, who became desperate to "Pearson proof" the process and give someone else a shot at winning. Wheeler changed the qualifying from two laps to three and then to four, hoping that somewhere in there Pearson would blow it. Finally, Wheeler tinkered with the track itself, taking the hump out of Turns 3 and 4.

Wheeler actually went so far as to tell Pearson, "I've got you now." Except he didn't. Pearson won yet another pole and afterwards made sure to tell Wheeler (and the press), "Humpy, you fixed the wrong turn."

In the end, there was nothing Wheeler could do to stop Pearson. It wasn't until he broke off with the Wood Brothers after the 1978 season that Pearson relinquished his record-breaking hold on the pole position in Charlotte.

David Pearson leads the way during action in the 1974 Charlotte World 600.

Busch the Younger Is the Youngest

● ● ● ● ● ● ● ● ●

Kyle Busch has always set a fast pace. On September 4, 2005, his speedy arrival at the finish line landed him in the record books.

Kyle began driving Legend Cars at age thirteen and winning championships in Las Vegas soon after. At sixteen Kurt Busch's younger brother won ten late model races, but he was banned from another race because it was sponsored by Marlboro cigarettes, which he was too young to even purchase. Soon afterwards, NASCAR raised its major-series age minimum to eighteen, knocking Busch out of a Craftsman Truck race even though he'd been the fastest qualifier.

Busch, who graduated high school early to pursue racing, competed in the American Speed Association until he was old enough for NASCAR. He joined the Hendrick racing team, and in 2004, while his brother was winning the Cup championship, Kyle won five Busch Series races. In February 2005, Busch, averaging 188.245 mph in his number 5 Chevy, became the youngest driver ever to earn a Cup pole position in the Auto Club 500 at California Speedway—even though he was too young to drink a beer made by the company that sponsors the pole trophy, Budweiser. He was still nineteen; the previous youngest winners, Brian Vickers and Donald Thomas, had both been twenty.

But the best was still to come. On September 4, back at the California Speedway for the Sony HD 500, Busch, at twenty years, four months, and two days, broke Thomas's five-decade-old mark, becoming the youngest driver ever to win. (Thomas was four days older in 1952 at his first win.)

Kyle Busch, driver of the #5 Hendrick Motorsports Kellogg's Chevrolet, celebrates after winning the NASCAR Nextel Cup Series Sony HD 500 on September 4, 2005 at California Speedway in Fontana, California.

It was a tough race on a wide track that allowed fast cars to pass easily—there were twelve different leaders overall. Tony Stewart led eight times for 56 laps, and Vickers led 95 laps; Busch grabbed the lead once early by passing his brother Kurt on Lap 82, but he really won it with a strong finish and some great improvising by his crew. During one of the eleven caution periods, Busch zoomed in for a pit stop, planning to change four tires, but he was too close to the wall, forcing crew chief Alan Gustafson to make the call to just change the right-side tires. But the miscalculation allowed Busch to get back out in third for the final-stretch drive with seven laps to go. With two laps left a three-car accident prompted a yellow flag and then Greg Biffle mounted one last charge, but Busch held him off.

After climbing out of his car, Busch announced he'd donate his winner's share to the Hurricane Katrina relief efforts, showing that he was not just a record-setting racer but a classy one at that.

Waltrip's Modern-Era Mark

● ● ● ● ● ● ● ● ●

The record holder for NASCAR Cup wins? Well, it depends on how you count. And that makes finding the record-breaking race a tricky business. But don't let the convoluted explanations about to come fool you—Darrell Waltrip's modern record is as legit as it gets and his place in NASCAR history is secure.

Waltrip the king of wins? What about the King? Richard Petty is the undisputed all-time champ with 200 first-place finishes, but the first 140 of those came before what NASCAR now calls the "modern" era. It's like Cy Young racking up most of his 511 wins in the nineteenth century. Back before 1972, the seasons were packed with races—Petty and his competitors would often race forty, or fifty, or even sixty times a year. More races, more chances to win...especially when you're the best in the business. Or, in the case of David Pearson, who won 60 of his 105 races before 1972, a close second best. (Here's the telling stat: in Petty's thirty-two full seasons he ran 1,140 races; in Waltrip's twenty-six full seasons, he ran 769.)

So Petty had only sixty modern wins and Pearson forty-five. Bobby Allison, who is cited as tied with Waltrip for third most, won just fifty-four of his eighty-four after 1972. That meant that Cale Yarborough was really the man Waltrip was chasing, though no one ever really took note of Waltrip passing him. Yarborough won his sixty-ninth race in 1985. Two years later, Waltrip snapped a twenty-seven-race winless streak and took home his seventieth crown at Martinsville in 1987.

But as record breakers go, that one's a bit unsatisfying—not because it was unheralded but because both Dale Earnhardt (who finished second at Martinsville that day) and Jeff Gordon have since passed that total.

So celebrating Waltrip should mean celebrating his final win, number eighty-four, on September 6, 1992, in the Mountain Dew Southern 500 at Darlington. This was seventeen years after Waltrip's first win and a decade since his peak when he won twelve times in both 1981 and 1982 in capturing two of his three Cup championships. (He also won in 1985.) It was just one week since his eighty-third win, in Bristol.

Waltrip, who'd been racing stock cars since he was sixteen—when he smashed up his 1936 Chevy coupe in his first try—didn't finish the 1992 Southern 500 either. But he didn't have to, since nobody did. Waltrip started fifth and ran about eighth or ninth for much of the day. Harry Gant led for 91 laps, Davey Allison for 72, Sterling Martin for 57, Mark Martin for 26, and Dale Jarrett for 21. Everyone knew rain was heading their way and Waltrip's crew did the best job of judging the weather. Waltrip timed it perfectly, staying out on the course when everyone else pitted, grabbing the lead just before the rain came. Waltrip's Chevrolet Lumina led for only six laps, but they were the right ones to be in front for—after 298 go-rounds (the last few were caution laps), NASCAR officials had to call the race, 69 laps shy of the end.

The Southern 500 was the one major race Waltrip had never won—in 1979 he'd lapped the field near the end but hit the wall—so he wasn't going to complain about the weather shortening his day. He was the winner, for the eighty-fourth time in his career—one more than Yarborough, and equal to Allison.

Darrell Waltrip (*center*) and crew celebrate after winning the 1992 Southern 500 at Darlington Raceway.

THE BEST ROOKIES OF THE YEAR

Once upon a time there were certain rules about rookies. Rookies did not win races. Rookies did not finish among the leaders in the NASCAR Cup race. Rookies did not pull attention-getting stunts... Tony Stewart rewrote the book on rookies.

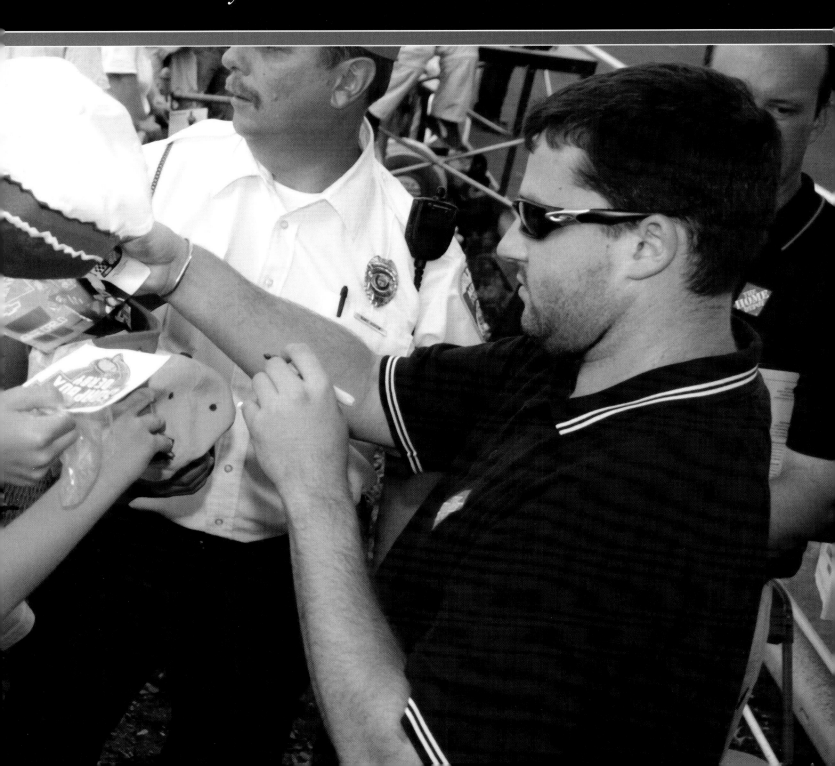

Tony Stewart, 1999

• • • • • • • • •

Once upon a time there were certain rules about rookies. Rookies did not finish among the leaders in the NASCAR championship. Rookies did not pull attention-getting stunts. Rookies did not throw public tantrums in the middle of a race.

Tony Stewart rewrote the book on rookies.

When Stewart came along in 1999, no freshman had won a race since Davey Allison in 1987 and only four had done so in four decades. The last rookie to finish in the top ten in points had been Jody Ridley in 1980. But the last in the top five? For that you had to go all the way back to James Hylton in 1966 (second) and Shorty Rollins in 1958 (fourth).

Then Tony Stewart entered the picture and won, not once (like Earl Ross, Dale Earnhardt, and Ron Bouchard), not twice (like Allison), but three times, and made history when he finished the season ranked fourth overall, thanks to twelve top five finishes, twenty-one top ten finishes, and an absolutely remarkable run of fifteen top ten finishes in a nineteen-week span. And by driving 1,090 total miles in the Indy 500 (finished ninth) and NASCAR's Coca-Cola 600 (finished fourth) on the same day and later angrily trying to reach into the car of another driver on the track, he made it clear he was not like any other driver.

Stewart, who began racing go-karts at age seven, came to NASCAR as a proven winner with three karting titles in his youth (his first at age eight, his first national title at age twelve), then followed by four USAC crowns (in 1995 he was the first USAC Triple Crown winner, capturing the National Midget, Sprint, and Silver Crown titles in one year) and, most notably, the 1996 IRL Rookie of the Year award and 1997 IRL championship. But in his one season driving for Joe Gibbs in the Busch Series in 1998, he raised the eyebrows of skeptics with his inconsistent performance—he ran twenty-two of thirty-one races with no wins and five top fives to finish twenty-first in the rankings. Not bad, of course, but certainly not an indicator that he was about to take the racing world by storm. Gibbs, however, had been impressed simply by the fact that Stewart was more interested in gaining experience than earning quick bucks in the Cup Series right away.

Like Davey Allison, Stewart turned some heads by earning a front-row spot at the Daytona 500, but he finished only twenty-eighth. Allison had finished similarly but followed up with a pole position the next week, and after

(*Overleaf*) **Tony Stewart signs memorabilia for his legions of fans.**

Tony Stewart #3 races at the Indianapolis 500 in Indianapolis, Indiana.

Tony Stewart streaks down the front stretch at Lowe's Motor Speedway in Concord, North Carolina en route to a 5th place finish in the Coca Cola 600 May 30, 1999. Earlier in the day Stewart had finished 9th in the Indianapolis 500 before jetting to North Carolina to compete in the later race.

eight races he had already won twice. Stewart had no such magic at the start, with two sixth-place finishes in those first eight races.

But at Talladega, everything changed. Stewart finished in the top ten—fifth, in fact—and soon it seemed like he would never leave. With only a few exceptions, week after week he was there, finishing in the top five as often as he was out of the top ten. The only question remaining was whether he could finish in front. He led for 127 laps at Dover and 118 at Loudon but his best opportunity seemed to come at the Goody's Headache Powder 500 in Bristol. He had the pole position and led for 225 laps, more than anyone else, before being

passed by the likes of winner Dale Earnhardt and Jeff Gordon and settling for a fifth-place finish. The next week, Stewart slumped to twelfth and it seemed that he might be just another talented rookie—ROTY to be sure, but not a record-setter.

Then came the short three-quarter-mile track at Richmond and the Exide 400. Stewart started in the second slot, and while he didn't lead start to finish— Jeff Gordon led for 56 laps before being downed by transmission troubles—he dominated the race, heading the pack for 333 of the 400 laps, including the final 144. An exhilarated Stewart left black marks on the pavement with the donuts he spun at the finish line, then drove a reverse victory lap while exuberantly pumping his arm out the window.

On October 3, NASCAR saw the other side of Stewart, the side that had earned the "Tony the Temper" nickname in the IRL. At Martinsville, Stewart, whose idol had been the tempestuous A. J. Foyt, bumped Kenny Irwin by mistake and reportedly sent an apology via radio. But they tangled a second

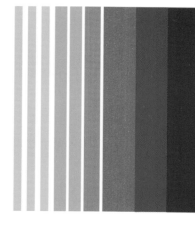

Indeed, despite all the attention during his great rookie campaign, Stewart remained true to himself, refusing to meet the press when he was frustrated after running out of gas...

time and then Irwin slammed Stewart into a wall. Stewart climbed out of his car and waited for Irwin to circle the track; after sarcastically applauding Irwin he hurled the heat shields from his racing boots at Irwin's car, then leaned his head in the window and shared some unpleasantries before Irwin pulled away. The display upset NASCAR officials—they fined Stewart $5,000— but many old-timers who preferred the hotheads of the past to the corporate stars of the present loved it. Indeed, despite all the attention during his great rookie campaign, Stewart remained true to himself, refusing to meet the press when he was frustrated after running out of gas cost him a win in New Hampshire but also spending spare time at dirt tracks or watching greyhound races or hanging out with his old friends.

On November 7 at Phoenix, the headlines were all positive again as the twenty-eight-year-old tied Davey Allison's rookie record by winning the Checker Auto Parts/Dura Lube 500. Stewart, who knew the one-mile flat track well from his USAC wins and IRL second-place finishes there, had the nerves and skill to drive loose and not slow down. After running out of fuel on Lap 89 he remembered what teammate Bobby Labonte had taught him about patience and slowly worked his way back before taking control and leading for 147 of the final 154 laps, cruising at the end with enough of a lead that he spent the last ten laps chatting on the radio with his crew en route to a race record average speed of 118.132 mph.

Tony Stewart, driver of the #20 Home Depot Chevrolet, celebrates winning the championship with his crew after the NASCAR Nextel Cup Ford 400 on November 20, 2005 at the Homestead-Miami Super speedway in Homestead, Florida.

The following week on a 1.5-mile track in Homestead at the Pennzoil 400, Stewart left Allison in his tracks, winning his third race as a rookie. And he did it in typical Stewart fashion—with a touch of controversy. Labonte, who had finished second and third in Stewart's two previous wins and who was fighting a losing battle with Dale Jarrett for the Cup championship, led for 174 of the 267 laps, but Stewart surged ahead at 228. After pit stops with less than twenty laps to go, the two found themselves door-to-door heading into Turn 3. Labonte tried pinching him down to grab control of the inside but Stewart wouldn't back down and rode hard until Labonte's car skittered sideways; both men had to fight for control of their cars but Stewart emerged on top. And that's where he finished (with Labonte second again).

Afterwards, Stewart apologized to his teammate but still stood his ground and spoke his mind. "I think [Labonte] respects the fact that I didn't just give it to him," he said. Indeed, at the end of that rookie season, Stewart had won the respect—and admiration—of just about everyone in NASCAR. But then, he was used to winning.

Matt Kenseth, 2000

● ● ● ● ● ● ● ● ● ●

To the casual NASCAR fan, it was pretty obvious who the front-runner for the 2000 Cup Rookie of the Year would be—after all, few racers started their engines with a more impressive pedigree than Dale Earnhardt Jr., whose father had earned the ROTY title in 1979.

But the experts knew another driver would approach the starting line with at least as good a chance to take home the crown. Matt Kenseth's dad did not bequeath him a sterling NASCAR legacy but he did play a pivotal role in his driving career. When Kenseth was thirteen his dad bought him a race car—but Kenseth was allowed only to work on it until he was sixteen. (Only his father could drive it.) By the time Matt was permitted behind the wheel, he had a taste for the hard work involved in racing and a deep understanding of everything that went on in his car.

In his home state of Wisconsin Kenseth won in just his third race, and by nineteen he was the youngest winner in ARTGO Challenge Series history; later he was the youngest victor in the Miller Genuine Draft National championships as well. By 1997, he was driving in NASCAR's Busch Series, where in just twenty-one starts he drove well enough to place second in Rookie of the Year points. The next year he won three races and landed second in overall points but also got a taste of the big time, subbing for Bill Elliott at Dover Downs and finishing sixth. With five additional Cup starts in 1999, Kenseth was heading into his rookie year with valuable experience, not to mention the backing of Jack Roush and a veteran crew, which helped prompt predictions that Kenseth would top Junior, despite not only Earnhardt's instant star status but also his back-to-back Busch Series championships.

Earnhardt won in just his seventh race, but Kenseth proved his consistency, with three top ten finishes in his first ten races compared to Earnhardt's

two. Earnhardt wowed everyone with his second win of the season at Richmond, in just the eleventh race, but again Kenseth kept pace, winning his own first the next time out at the Coca-Cola 600 at Lowe's Motor Speedway and finishing second the very next week. Earnhardt failed to crack the top ten after his thirteenth race but Kenseth just kept going and going, racking up three top ten finishes in four races beginning at the Pocono Raceway, then adding back-to-back top tens at Lowe's and Talladega in his twenty-ninth and thirtieth races. For good measure, Kenseth finished the season's last race, in Atlanta, in a place he'd become quite comfortable—the top ten. His ninth-place showing was his fourteenth such finish of the year.

Both drivers would go on to achieve great glory—Kenseth would capture the Cup championship in 2003—but in their rookie year there was no doubt who was number one.

Ron Bouchard, 1981

• • • • • • • • •

Heading into the final lap of the Talladega 500 in August 1981, three drivers were pushing hard, the race undecided: Darrell Waltrip, on his way to that year's Cup title and to becoming the all-time modern wins leader; Terry Labonte, who had won the Southern 500 the previous year and his first pole position in 1981; and Ron Bouchard, a thirty-two-year-old nobody of a rookie in just his eleventh Cup race.

The times were different—these days it seems that every year at least one rookie, backed by top teams and deep-pocketed sponsors, pulls out a win (Tony Stewart, Dale Earnhardt Jr., Ryan Newman, Matt Kenseth, Kevin Harvick, Jamie McMurray). But back then, it almost never happened. From the start of the

modern era in 1972 through 1998, only five racers accomplished the feat: Earl Ross (1974), future legends Dale Earnhardt (1979) and Davey Allison (1987), and two newcomers in 1981. One was Morgan Shepherd, who'd win in his fifteenth race and finish as Rookie of the Year runner-up.

The other was Ron Bouchard, who thrilled the crowd by accelerating past both Waltrip and Labonte with just a few yards remaining to pull out a stunning win at Talladega—it was the quickest Cup win for any rookie in history (although McMurray later shattered that mark, winning in just his second Cup race).

Despite it happening so early in his Cup career, this triumph was a long time coming. Bouchard's enthusiasm for racing had spurred his father, who owned a trucking company, to sponsor a local driver, Pete Salvatore. When Salvatore fell ill, the fourteen-year-old Bouchard made his debut behind the wheel at Brookline Speedway in Massachusetts. Later in high school he began racing frequently, and afterwards he found success and repeatedly won in NASCAR Modified races at tracks like Connecticut's Stafford Speedway.

Still, it wasn't until 1981 that Bouchard made the jump to the Cup series.

It would take until 2000 before two rookies (Matt Kenseth and Dale Jr.) again each won in a single year.

Bouchard, whose brother Ken won Rookie of the Year in 1988, never won another Cup race after his fantastic finish. But the thirty-two-year-old was consistent enough in his twenty-two races in 1981—landing in the top ten more than half the time with twelve all told, with five top five finishes and one pole position—that he finished twenty-first in points and, more significantly, edged out Shepherd in the Rookie of the Year race, with 392 rookie points to Shepherd's 378.

Not bad for an old man.

Jamie McMurray, 2003

• • • • • • • • • •

In the race for the 2003 Cup Series Rookie of the Year, Jamie McMurray proved himself a fast starter and a slow starter. But what mattered most was his strong finish.

First, the fast: McMurray got a head start in terms of proving himself when Sterling Martin was injured in 2002. McMurray was designated as the pinch hitter for Chip Ganassi Racing's number 40 Dodge over the final six events of the Cup season. McMurray, who had broken out in the Busch Series that year with two wins,

fourteen top ten finishes, and the sixth-best points total. He then startled everyone by winning just his second Cup race, something no driver had ever done before. But he also proved his moment of triumph at the UAW-GM Quality 500 at Lowe's Motor Speedway in Charlotte that October was no fluke by adding two more top fifteen finishes.

The Joplin, Missouri, native was hoping for an

Jamie McMurray, driver of the #42 Chip Ganassi Racing Havoline celebrates pole position after qualifying for the NASCAR Winston Cup Ford 400 on November 14, 2003 at Homestead-Miami Speedway in Homestead, Florida.

accelerated start in 2003 but he struggled throughout the first half of the season with his consistency. Durability, by contrast, was never a problem—McMurray would be one of only two rookies, along with teammate Casey Mears, to compete in all thirty-six Cup races in 2003. But McMurray also drove in nineteen Busch Series races, posting two wins and nine top ten finishes.

In the Nextel Cup season opener at Daytona, McMurray started in the nineteenth position but finished just thirty-first. But in his next race at Rockingham he again showed his potential when he earned the seventh starting slot and reached the finish

line in fifth place—he and Greg Biffle would be the only two rookies to finish in the top five even once. But while Biffle was impressive early on, McMurray seemed attached to a yo-yo, not a car. He started twelfth in Las Vegas but finished thirty-second, then added two more top tens in his first ten races but scuffled through the next go-round at Daytona, starting eighth and finishing just thirty-seventh while Biffle won it all, before bouncing back with an eighth-place finish in Chicago.

Then halfway through the season, McMurray seemed to hit the top of his learning curve. In his last sixteen races, he placed in the top ten in half of them, including two third-place finishes (Indy and Bristol), a fourth (Darlington), and a ninth in the season's final race in Homestead, where he'd also earned his first pole position. McMurray, who finished thirteenth in overall Cup points, was the top rookie in fourteen of his last sixteen races, leaving no doubt at season's end about who deserved Rookie of the Year.

Kevin Harvick, 2001

• • • • • • • • •

Kevin Harvick was not the first kid in the world whose parents bought him a set of wheels as a graduation present...except that his mom and dad were celebrating his graduation from kindergarten.

Admittedly, it was not a car but a go-kart, but still that might seem a bit extravagant to some folks. In this case, however, it was a particularly prophetic purchase. Harvick plunged headfirst into the world of racing, showing from the beginning the perseverance and skills that would make him NASCAR's 2001 Cup Rookie of the Year.

Harvick won seven National championships and two Grand National championships in ten years on the go-kart circuit before graduating to a limited schedule on a regional NASCAR division during high school. Finally, in 1995 he drove a full season in the Featherlite Southwest Series and raced off with the Rookie of the Year award.

That helped encourage Harvick to skip one last graduation—from college—and leave behind Bakersfield Junior College in 1997 for a life in racing. He quickly demonstrated he'd made the right choice, winning the 1998 Winston West Series championship and then winning three Busch Series races in 2000 en route to another Rookie of the Year award.

But the big one, the one all drivers dream of— the coveted Cup Series Rookie of the Year award— was still to come.

In 2001, Harvick put together one of the most remarkable, and certainly one of the busiest, years of his career.

On February 28, Harvick married DeLana Linville. But he had no time for a honeymoon. He was, after all, driving a full Busch Series schedule and he was favored to win it all. He won five races along the way, but while he kept his day job in the Busch, he also found himself

Kevin Harvick, driving a Chevrolet Monte Carlo #29 for Richard Childress Racing, speeds down the track during the Food City 500, part of the NASCAR Winston Cup Series at the Bristol Motor Speedway in Bristol, Tennessee.

with the opportunity of a lifetime. After Dale Earnhardt died in the Daytona 500, car owner Richard Childress asked him to take the Intimidator's place in the Cup series.

Sure, Harvick said. And so in his spare time he won two Cup races, posted sixteen top ten finishes, and ended up ninth in the points race. Harvick was the first driver ever to go full-time on both the Busch and Cup circuits—seventy races in one season. He was also the first person to win Busch Series championship and the Cup Rookie of the Year in the same season.

No wonder this guy earned the nickname "Happy."

Ryan Newman, 2002
• • • • • • • • • •

There are impressive Rookie of the Year campaigns...and then there's Ryan Newman.

Numbers can never tell the whole story, of course, but it's impossible to look at Newman's stats from 2002 and not be a bit awed. After all, for sheer consistency in terms of accomplishment in his very first go-round, Newman's record outshines the freshman efforts of drivers ranging from Dale Earnhardt to Davey Allison to Jeff Gordon to Kasey Kahne.

Newman won one race, at the New Hampshire International Speedway in September, but more significantly, he earned a record six pole positions (breaking Allison's 1987 mark), finished in the top five a whopping fourteen times (second only to superstar Tony Stewart for the season), and in the Top 10 twenty-two times—all of those totals are more than any other rookie driver.

Newman, a decidedly new breed of driver, graduated from Purdue University with a degree in vehicle structure engineering and a love of new technology.

Yet what's most astonishing is that for much of the 2002 season Newman wasn't even the frontrunner for the award—Jimmie Johnson, who won three races, seemed to have the Rookie of the Year prize wrapped up. Johnson burst off to a faster start, and by June he was proclaimed the consensus favorite for Rookie of the Year, even stirring

Ryan Newman, driver of the #12 Alltel Ford, celebrates winning The Winston NASCAR event at the Lowe's Motor Speedway in Concord, North Carolina on May 18, 2002.

up the possibility that he might actually win the NASCAR Cup Series. By then he'd already amassed three poles and two superspeedway wins and was second in points; early in the fall he actually was the overall point leader. Newman had four "did not finish" races early on and languished down around sixteenth in points. But this was a tortoise-and-the-hare kind of race, and Newman found his groove and hit the gas, peaking with that win in New Hampshire over red-hot Kurt Busch and Tony Stewart.

At season's end, Johnson, because of his three wins, finished with 4,600 points in fifth place, making him just the second rookie, after Stewart in 1999, to finish in the Top 5 in points. But Newman was right on his tail at 4,593, and since the rookie crown is based on a driver's seventeen best finishes, the prize went not to the hare Johnson but to the tortoise, the more consistent Newman.

Davey Allison, 1987

● ● ● ● ● ● ● ● ●

Davey Allison was born to racing—literally. He arrived in 1961 on the eve of the Daytona 500 in which his father Bobby Allison would make his debut. Davey began helping out in the family business at the age of twelve and completed high school four months early so he could start working full-time at Bobby Allison Racing. (A high school diploma was his father's requirement.)

The younger Allison began racing in 1979 in a Chevy Nova that he and his friends had built themselves. He earned a win in just his sixth start, with Dad watching proudly. By the time he worked his way up from Limited Sportsman events through Grand American, ARCA, Busch Grand National, and other circuits to the big time of the NASCAR Cup circuit, he had more than proved that he was not just coasting on his father's name—in 1983 he'd won a superspeedway pole and the race at Talladega, in 1984 he was the ARCA Rookie of the Year, and in his first few Cup efforts in 1985 and '86 he pulled off two Top 10 finishes.

In 1987, Allison started just twenty-two of twenty-nine Cup races in his first full season, but was so overwhelmingly successful that he still raced off with Rookie of the Year honors. After all, he nabbed his first pole position in the season's second race, and

In 1987, Allison started just 22 of 29 Winston Cup races in his first full season but was so overwhelmingly successful that he still raced off with Rookie of the Year honors.

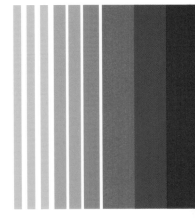

thanks to his dazzling 209 miles per hour qualifying run, he became the first rookie ever to sit in the front row for the Daytona 500. Allison finished the year with a rookie record of eight front-row starts, including five pole positions. But he didn't just start strong—there was more substance than sizzle as Allison became the first rookie to win two superspeedway races (at Talladega and Dover) while also finishing second three times by two seconds or less. Overall he finished in the Top 10 ten times and despite his low number of races he was twenty-first in points.

Unfortunately, after a grand start to his sophomore

Davey Allison celebrates his 1987 victory at Talladega.

season—Bobby and Davey Allison finished one-two at Daytona in 1988—tragedy struck the Allison family again and again. First, Bobby got a flat tire in the first lap at the Pocono Raceway, slammed into a wall, then was hit by another driver—a devastating crash that ended his career. Davey was on the track that day. After several more successful years, Davey Allison's life turned dark in 1992 when his grandfather died, he endured several crashes, and was hospitalized twice; worst of all his brother Clifford died in a one-car crash at Michigan International Speedway. Then in 1993, Davey died from injuries suffered when his helicopter crashed at Talladega Superspeedway. But even though his life and his career were cut short, Allison will always be remembered for that magical rookie season.

Jeff Gordon, 1993
● ● ● ● ● ● ● ● ●

Jeff Gordon? Well *of course* he was Rookie of the Year. Anything less would have been unacceptable, both for the relentless, determined twenty-two-year-old future champion and for the NASCAR world that had heaped such great expectations upon him.

Inspired and prodded by his stepfather John Bickford (a former motorcycle racer), Gordon was into quarter-midget racers before he was five, winning thirty-five races by the age of seven in suburban California. He added go-karts to his repertoire and hundreds of wins to his résumé by age thirteen when he turned to sprint cars. So it was no surprise that by 1990 he was the USAC Midget champion, and in his first year after shifting from open wheel to NASCAR he was the 1991 Grand National Rookie of the Year at age twenty. The following year he won three races and a record eleven poles, leading all comers in earnings. He was ready for the big time and the NASCAR Cup stage was ready for him.

Nineteen ninety-three was the best of times and the worst of times for NASCAR. On the one hand, NASCAR was really coming into its own as a mainstream sport, drawing more televised events, higher ratings, and more corporate interest, gaining momentum for the explosion in the sport's appeal that would follow at decade's end. On the other hand, Richard Petty had just retired (his final race the previous fall was Gordon's Cup debut) and in '93 both Davey Allison and Alan Kulwicki died, in helicopter and plane crashes, respectively.

Gordon helped fill the superstar void, finishing fourteenth in points and displaying the clean-cut boyish charm, naked ambition and confidence, and business savvy that gave him such commercial appeal and NASCAR a much brighter future. One NASCAR official enthusiastically dubbed him the "Shaquille O'Neal of NASCAR."

The hype surrounding Gordon was so great that some grumbled that he was a disappointment because he didn't win any races (one of only three ROTYs in this list not to score a victory). Even Gordon confessed to feeling let down.

Still, he ran far ahead of the competition for Rookie of the Year, after he finished fifth in his first Daytona 500 and second both in Charlotte and in Michigan; in thirty races he finished in the Top 5 seven times and the Top 10 eleven times. Along the way he attracted attention from the mainstream press and a slew of new fans; he joined veterans Dale Earnhardt and Rusty Wallace on the McDonald's all-star team and prompted a set of collector cards with Earnhardt titled *The Champion and the Challenger,* and soon landed on Frosted Mini-Wheats boxes.

A year later Gordon began winning, most notably in the first Brickyard 400 at Indianapolis Motor Speedway. Soon no one could doubt that he was for real.

Jeff Gordon races in his Dupont #24 car against
the Dale Earnhardt #3 Goodwrench car
during the Daytona 500 at Daytona Speedway on
February 14, 1993 in Daytona Beach, Florida.

Kasey Kahne, 2004

• • • • • • • • •

Kasey Kahne's Nextel Cup debut did not make headlines.

Engine failure in the Daytona 500 isn't considered big news. But just one week later at Rockingham, he thrilled the crowd by staying neck and neck with 2003 Cup champ Matt Kenseth to the very end, losing by 0.01 seconds.

Still, it was just his second Cup race ever, and given his good but not great showing in the Busch Series, many thought Rockingham a fluke. But

In the middle of the season he nailed five top five finishes over an eight-race span; then from weeks 33 to 35, Kahne added three straight top fives to his résumé, giving him thirteen on the year, the second most ever behind Stewart.

Kahne, who'd dumped Ford before the season for the Evernham Motorsports Dodge team where he replaced the legendary Bill Elliott, silenced his skeptics with great speed. One week later, the nervy Kahne earned his first pole position in Las Vegas and again breathed down Kenseth's neck all the way to the finish line, keeping ahead of Tony Stewart and finishing a close second, just 3.4 seconds behind.

Suddenly, everyone knew that Kahne, who'd shown great poise in two tight situations, was the real deal. The buzz only grew louder when he finished third the next week in Atlanta, then sped

to a pole position in the following race at Darlington. Two weeks later in Texas, he was second again, this time to Elliott Sadler by a mere 0.028 seconds.

Just seven weeks into the season, Kahne was suddenly a candidate not just for ROTY but for the NASCAR Cup crown. Although he wouldn't be able to maintain that blistering pace for the whole season—he'd finish thirteenth in points—he did generate plenty of buzz when *People* magazine named him one of America's 50 Hottest Bachelors.

Kahne was the first ROTY since 1998 not to win a race. He was leading at Dover before spinning out in an oil slick, which led to a wreck when officials did not throw a caution flag quickly enough. In Chicago Kahne was also in first until Stewart clipped the back of his car and caused a wreck in the final mile. But what was so impressive was how consistent he remained after his smoking start. In the middle of the season he nailed five Top 5 finishes over an eight-race span; then from weeks 33 to 35, Kahne added three straight top fives to his résumé, giving him thirteen on the year, the second most ever behind Stewart.

On the track, Kahne, who also earned eight front-row starts, may have suffered from close-but-no-cigar syndrome in the Cup races, but he did win back-to-back races at Darlington and Miami in the only two NASCAR Craftsman Truck Series events he drove in. More important was his one big Cup triumph in 2004: he won the Rookie of the Year Award in a cakewalk by 120 points over Brendan Gaughan, making the twenty-four-year-old the youngest winner since Jeff Gordon in 1993.

Kasey Kahne leads the pack in his #9 Dodge Dealers/UAW Dodge Intrepid at the start of the Carolina Dodge Dealers 400 on March 21, 2004 at the Darlington Motor Speedway in Darlington, South Carolina.

Dale Earnhardt, 1980

• • • • • • • • • •

Early in the 1979 season, a twenty-seven-year-old rookie by the name of Dale Earnhardt found himself heading into the final laps at the Southeastern 500 at Bristol International Raceway in Tennessee locked in a tight battle with more proven drivers Bobby Allison and Darrell Waltrip. Although only three other rookies had ever won a race and this was just the seventh race of the year and just his sixteenth NASCAR Cup race overall, Earnhardt pulled away for the victory.

Just a few weeks later, Earnhardt, already gaining a reputation for pushing the limits of speed, blew a tire while leading at Pocono. The crash required that he be airlifted out by helicopter and left him with two broken collarbones, a concussion, and severe neck and chest bruises. He was sidelined for four races. David Pearson filled in driving Osterlund's Chevy and nearly made everyone forget that rookie, finishing second at Talladega, fourth at Michigan, and then first in the Southern 500. But Earnhardt returned the following week as if he'd never been away, winning the pole at Richmond and then finishing fourth in the race.

Experienced rivals like Waltrip and Allison, a painful accident, an impressive run by his substitute—nothing could slow this rookie down. It was safe to say that Dale Earnhardt would not be intimidated.

Such icy poise was not totally surprising given that his father, Ralph, the 1958 Late Model Sportsman champ, was nicknamed "Ironheart" (he liked to toy with opponents), and that when Ralph died of a heart attack in 1973, Dale (who some dubbed "Ironhead" for his stubbornness early on before he became "the Intimidator") worked through his grief by working on his cars.

By 1975, the high school dropout had made his Cup debut, but he continued to struggle, going deep in debt as his marriage was falling apart. Then Rod Osterlund gave him a shot in 1978 and Earnhardt finished fourth at the Dixie 500 in Atlanta; when Osterland's regular driver, Dave Marcis, left, Osterland tapped Earnhardt for 1979.

It was a talented class of rookies, and Earnhardt went down to the wire against Joe Millikan, Harry Gant, and Terry Labonte, but his eleven top five finishes got him close, and his ninth-place finish in the season finale at Ontario put him over.

He also finished seventh overall in points, which was especially impressive considering the four-week layoff. But it wasn't good enough for Earnhardt, who proved in 1980 that there's no such thing as a sophomore jinx when he became the first Rookie of the Year to follow that up with a Cup championship in his second season.

Nothing could slow this young driver, prompting fellow driver Buddy Baker to declare that Earnhardt "has more damn nerve than a sore tooth."

Petty and Pearson: Legends Collide at the 1976 Daytona 500

● ● ● ● ● ● ● ● ● ●

Richard Petty wasn't feeling much like a defending NASCAR Cup champion with five Daytona 500 notches on his belt. Didn't feel like a King, either, when he rolled into that Florida racing complex in February of 1976. Twelve days of intravenous feeding and assorted ulcer treatments at the hospital tend to shake the glitter off even the most exciting times. It was the price he paid for being at the very top of the NASCAR pyramid.

David Pearson was almost the exact opposite. A South Carolina Zen master years before anyone ever visualized that concept, he was so alarmingly calm in virtually every situation imaginable as to make others nervous.

But these two opposites shared a profession and a passion, and at high speeds they definitely attracted one

Against the backdrop of the Daytona 500 and Bicentennial of 1976, the legendary crash of Petty (#43) and Pearson unfolds in Florida.

another, usually as they approached the checkered flag. Fifty-seven times in the previous thirteen seasons they had finished one-two in Cup races, with Pearson winning twenty-nine of those duels.

But in the days before that Bicentennial 500, it was three other drivers caught in the spotlight...and just plain *caught*. A. J. Foyt had his pole-winning speed of 187.477 mph thrown out after officials discovered he had used a nitrous oxide injection to boost power to the Chevy's engine during his qualifying run. Darrell Waltrip, with the second fastest qualifying speed, was next to get pinched, again for having a hidden bottle of laughing gas. And qualifier number three Dave Marcis had *his* time disallowed because of illegal radiator modifications intended to increase the track-hugging ability of his car.

Officials and especially NASCAR president Bill France did not find anything funny about Nitrous-Gate. Foyt was livid and protested the accusation. Waltrip and Marcis were silent and sheepish. All three were sent to the back of the pack, and when the green flag fell for the eighteenth Daytona 500, it was the Chevrolet of a veteran Midwestern driver named Ramo Stott that started from the pole.

But Stott wasn't there for long. As the pace picked up the natural leaders and stars of the series moved to the front. Hard-charging Buddy Baker led for a time, but the engine in his Ford Torino exploded on Lap 83. Waltrip's Monte Carlo lived up to Chevrolet's reputation for unquestioned speed coupled with questionable durability and expired just four laps later. On Lap 143 Foyt was the next front-runner to blow. Defending Daytona 500 leader Benny Parsons was also in contention, but as the race wound down there were two cars everyone knew would battle for the victory: the blue-and-red number 43 Petty Enterprises Dodge and the number 21 Wood Brothers Mercury with David Pearson behind the wheel.

Petty took the lead with thirteen laps to go, much earlier than anyone anticipated. Pearson kept the Mercury in tight, right on the bumper of his rival. When one went low, so did the other. If Petty went a little higher, Pearson followed. Mirror images, two of the best minds in racing playing a 180 mph game of chess, both trying to see ahead to a final move that would allow him to claim the finish line following Lap 200.

As the two drivers flew into the last lap the jockeying increased. Pearson searched for enough of an opening to pass the STP Dodge; Petty, meanwhile, did his best to stay directly in front of the Mercury. In Turn 4 Petty tried to make another course correction but bumped Pearson, and both cars fishtailed into the wall.

Petty's Dodge caromed off and slid down the track. He eventually stopped, engine dead, in the tri-oval grass about twenty yards from the finish line. As Pearson was sliding back down toward the inside wall he was clipped by the car driven by veteran Joe Frasson, a nudge that turned Pearson around, back *toward* the start-finish line. Through it all and true to form, Mr. Calm kept his cool. As the incident was unfolding, completely out of view of his crew in the pits, a member of Pearson's Wood Brothers team instinctively yelled a warning via radio: "There's a wreck off Turn 4!" And Pearson coolly replied, "Yeah I know, I'm in it." He had had the presence of mind during the accident to push in his clutch and keep the engine turning.

Slowly, *oh so slowly*, Pearson chugged his battered Mercury to the finish line. Some say 20 mph, others claim it was more like 30 or 40 mph, but there is no doubt it is by far the slowest finish-line speed for a winner of the Great American Race. Petty's crew scrambled to assist their stalled boss, but it was all over. Except for the memories of what many claim was a truly defining moment for the sport.

It was Pearson's only Daytona 500 victory. Petty would go on to win two more, for a grand total of seven. But the King is unashamedly the first to admit, "The race I'll be remembered most for—and the one I'll remember most myself—was one I lost."

David Pearson poses with his wrecked race car in victory lane after an accident with Richard Petty on the final lap of the 1976 Daytona 500. Petty could not restart his car and Pearson crawled to the finish line.

1979 Daytona 500: The Rumble in the Infield

• • • • • • • • • •

With the current-day avalanche of media coverage it's difficult to imagine a time when NASCAR racing wasn't one of the country's most popular sporting events, commanding hours of weekly television time.

However, before February 18, 1979, there had not been a live coast-to-coast NASCAR TV broadcast. There were occasional regional broadcasts if you lived in or around the Southeast, or stock car snippets cut-and-pasted between ice skating and cliff diving on *Wide World of Sports*. But after years of courting network television, NASCAR president Bill France was finally able to convince CBS to take a great leap of faith and show the '79 season-opening Daytona 500 live.

With a good portion of the East blanketed by a heavy weekend snowfall, a much larger than anticipated audience tuned in. The vast majority were seeing their first ever live NASCAR broadcast,

Bobby Allison holds race driver Cale Yarborough's foot after Yarborough kicked him following an argument February 18, 1979 when Yarborough stopped his car during the final lap of the Daytona 500. Allison's brother Donnie was involved in a wreck with Yarborough on the final lap which made brother Bobby stop.

and they were treated to an exciting contest from the moment the green flag fell.

Cale Yarborough, who the previous season had set a NASCAR record by capturing his third consecutive NASCAR Cup championship, was clearly the car to beat. But less than a quarter of the way into the race there was trouble. Donnie Allison swerved while trying to avoid a slower car, and directly behind him Yarborough—and Allison's own brother Bobby—were forced off the track and plowed through an infield soaked by a morning rainstorm. Yarbrough's Oldsmobile got the worst of it: repairs took long enough to cost him four laps and seemingly a chance at winning.

Still, never underestimate a great driver in a fast car, especially when it's Cale Yarborough facing a challenge. Using every ounce of his ability, every inch of the track, and some terrific pit strategy, he was able to get back behind leader Donnie Allison and the lapped car of brother Bobby for a final sprint to the finish.

"I made up my mind that he would have to pass me up high," Donnie Allison said. "When he tried to pass me low, he went off the track." Allison pinched Yarborough's Olds down to the apron, but Yarborough would not back off. The cars touched, and then slammed into each other again—at 185 mph!—and careened into the outside wall before sliding back down to the infield. Richard Petty and Darrell Waltrip, running third and fourth almost a mile back, were suddenly and improbably crossing the finish line one-two.

Bobby Allison completed his final lap and drove back to check on his brother. Yarborough, already out of his crumpled car, yelled at Bobby and took a swing at him through the race car window. Donnie tried to restrain Yarborough as Bobby emerged from his car. And then the real fireworks began. The three drivers started wrestling around in the infield mud. Bobby at one point had Yarborough by the throat. And it was all played out for the national TV audience.

"The Daytona 500 Fight" was the number one topic the next day at water coolers and lunch tables from California to Maine. And NASCAR racing began to scale its way up the ladder to major sporting-event status.

2001 Daytona 500: A Legend Is Lost

•••••••••

Michael Waltrip wasn't sure where he *would* be, but was fairly certain that without Dale Earnhardt it *wouldn't* be flying through Turn 4 in the lead on the last lap of the Daytona 500. This was Waltrip's first run in a Dale Earnhardt Incorporated car, and with Junior glued to his back bumper and their boss Dale in third, all Waltrip had to do was keep the wheels straight for another half-mile.

In the broadcast booth, rookie announcer Darrell Waltrip was losing it...his composure and his objectivity. The three-time NASCAR Cup champion added expert analysis and high-profile star quality to NASCAR's new $2.8 billion television package, but seeing his six-foot-five, 200-pound baby brother just a

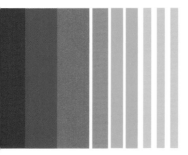

But in the instant it took for Dale Earnhardt to tangle with another car and shoot up the track into the outside wall, one of the brightest, most improbable moments became the most tragic in NASCAR history.

straightaway from breaking a 462-race winless streak and crowning the Waltrips the only siblings with wins in the Great American Race was almost more than he could stand. Ol' DW hollering, "Go Mikey!!!!!" just seemed to fit.

Seconds before the checkered flag all the elements were in place for a backslapping, one-for-the-ages Daytona 500 that everyone would cheer about for years to come: *The Intimidator keeps the field at bay so his newest employee and his son can go one-two in the biggest race of the season!* But in the instant it took for Dale Earnhardt to tangle with another car and shoot up the track into the outside wall, one of the brightest, most improbable moments became the most tragic in NASCAR history.

Emergency workers, hoping for a miracle, immediately transported the gravely injured driver to nearby Halifax Medical Center. The trauma team

Ken Schrader (36) slams into Dale Earnhardt (3) during the Daytona 500 Sunday afternoon February 18, 2001 at the Daytona International Speedway in Daytona Beach, Florida. Earnhardt, the driver people either loved or hated, was killed in the crash.

worked frantically, but after twenty-two agonizing minutes realized their attempt at resuscitation was futile.

On Sunday, February 18, 2001, Dale Earnhardt was pronounced dead at 5:16 p.m. EST.

It was one of those where-were-you-when-you-heard-about-it moments. An unbelieving shock momentarily paralyzed the NASCAR nation. Heartbroken fans stood shoulder to shoulder at impromptu shrines in Earnhardt's hometown of Kannapolis, North Carolina, and seventeen miles away in Mooresville at the DEI complex. Memorials spread to racetracks big and small from Portland, Maine, to Portland, Oregon. "It's like losing a friend, even though I've never met him," said one grieving South Carolina fan. "Dale Earnhardt was what made NASCAR NASCAR. He showed us that it's okay to be a regular guy."

The drivers, a superstitious bunch who tend to look long and hard in the opposite direction when tragedy invades the racetrack, were similarly shaken to the core. "It was like the day Elvis died, or Princess

Diana or John Kennedy or Martin Luther King," Darrell Waltrip said. "Dale Earnhardt was not just a guy who drove a race car. He was a hero all over the world and the sport will never be the same. He was the last connection to guys like Fireball Roberts, Junior Johnson, and Richard Petty."

1988 Daytona 500: Allison versus Allison

• • • • • • • • •

NASCAR is a business, a *big* business. But more importantly, NASCAR is a family business. And that was never more apparent than during the 1988 Daytona 500 when Bobby Allison and his son Davey turned the Great American Race into a family picnic.

Since 1959, the contest at the famous Florida track had been increasing in stature. Some three decades later it commanded comparisons to an inverted Super Bowl, coming not at the end but at the beginning of each NASCAR campaign. Daytona was by far the biggest stage the sport had to offer; drivers chased the largest purse of the year in the fastest cars their teams could build.

Father and son compete on the sport's greatest stage, the Daytona 500.

Or at least they had until 1988. Engine advancement and aerodynamic innovations had nudged speeds well above the 200 mph mark. In an attempt to slow the cars down, the use of restrictor plates that cut the air flow into the carburetor—and therefore the horsepower—was mandated for use during races on the two biggest NASCAR tracks, beginning with the 1988 Great American Race.

The featured drivers were a pair of three-time series champions, each chomping at the bit to win his first Daytona 500 crown: Darrell Waltrip and Dale Earnhardt. But the ghost of past disappointments bit them both. Waltrip was in the lead when the engine in his Chevrolet went south with 14 laps remaining. Earnhardt, on the other hand, was never a contender and felt he had been hamstrung with the new power-sapping restrictor plate. "It's a lot more dangerous out there than when we were running at 210," he said. "I bumped and got bumped more than at Richmond." The race became an Allison versus Allison affair over the final ten laps, father in the lead with the son he taught so well in hot pursuit. When it was all said and done, Davey's Thunderbird just didn't have the top-end *ooomph* to pull off the last-lap pass, and Bobby Allison—at age fifty the oldest winner ever—wound up with the third Daytona 500 victory of his career.

Afterwards, the two Allisons shared a microphone during the post-race interview normally reserved for winners only. "My parents were a real inspiration for me and now I'm racing against my son," Bobby said. "It was a great race and I am very proud of him. He's a fine young man and a fine competitor. He drove the wheels off the car all day."

Said Davey, happy with finishing second behind his father but nonetheless a true racer, "I spent the whole day trying to figure out a way to win."

1993 Daytona 500: "Come on Dale, Go Baby Go!"

● ● ● ● ● ● ● ● ●

Every year since 1979, mid-February was supposed to be THE time, and the 2.5-mile high-banked oval known as Daytona International Speedway was supposed to be THE place.

This is where Dale Earnhardt was going to catch up to the dream, outrun the bad luck, bad breaks, and bad karma, and jettison the frustration that incrementally increased with each and every dreadful hand he was dealt during the Daytona 500.

Would the Great American Hero—and anti-hero—ever win the Great American Race?

Earnhardt made a very good case for himself in the preliminary events leading up to the '93 race and even went so far as to say, "I feel better about my chances to win this race than I have about any 500 in a long time."

So no one was surprised when Dale finally arrived in Victory Lane.

Except nearly everyone was expecting it to be Dale Earnhardt, not Dale Jarrett.

Jarrett is the son of two-time series champion Ned Jarrett, who had become a popular race announcer for NASCAR radio and television broadcasts. As a second-generation driver, DJ was trying his best to establish his own racing credentials. After breaking his

0-for-128 winless streak with a victory at Michigan two years earlier, he was once again feeling the pressure and hearing the whispers. Except from his father. "People tell me I often don't give him the credit he deserves," the elder Jarrett said, "but I don't want to appear biased."

As the '93 race progressed, Earnhardt looked to be on the way to victory. But Jarrett stayed close and by the last lap was running door-to-door with the Intimidator as they moved together into the final turn.

It was that moment when the elder Jarrett let objectivity escape through the TV broadcast-booth

Dale Jarrett, driver of the #18 Interstate Batteries car, leads the pack during the 35th Daytona 500 at Daytona International Speedway on February 14, 1993 in Daytona Beach, Florida.

window with a burst of verbal excitement, enthusiasm, and parental pride so genuine that no one faulted him for it.

"Come on Dale, go baby go...all right, come on...I know he's gone to the floorboard...he can't do any more...come on, take her to the inside, don't let him get on the inside of you comin' around the turn...here he comes...it's Dale and Dale as they come off Turn 4... you know who I'm pulling for is Dale Jarrett...bring her to the inside Dale, don't let him get down there...he's gonna make it, Dale's gonna win the Daytona 500! All right!"

Dale Jarrett was understandably elated, and almost as excited as his father. "I sat in my parents' car when I was eight and nine years old, pretending I was driving in the Daytona 500," the thirty-six-year-old driver said. "Of course, I won every time back then. Now I really have won it."

Meanwhile, standing once again in disappointingly familiar territory, Dale Earnhardt did his best to be philosophical. "I've lost this thing fifteen times, but I think tomorrow will still be Monday."

1981 Daytona 500: A Win Fit for a King
● ● ● ● ● ● ● ● ●

There are seven seas, seven days of the week, seven sacraments, seven deadly sins, seven wonders of the world, and seven innings before you stretch.

But there is just one driver who has seven Daytona 500 wins on his fit-for-a-King racing résumé.

Richard Petty began his career in 1958 and soon moved into the spotlight with hard-charging victories on paved tracks, dirt tracks, long tracks, and short tracks from one end of NASCAR's traveling circuit to the other. But in addition to his seven championships and record-setting 200 career wins, Petty's royal status is very much tied to his proficiency—no, make that his *domination*—in the biggest and most important race of each season.

In the King's first two Daytona 500 victories (1964 and 1966) he was clearly the fastest on the track. During the next decade Petty would combine his considerable driving talent with great cars, smart pit strategies, and amazing good luck—plus the bad luck that bit some of the best drivers in each of those fields—for wins in '71, '73, '74, and

The King rides to victory.

'79. He was a six-time winner when no other driver had more than two victories.

But number seven seemed to be slipping just out of Petty's reach. Gunning Buddy Baker, still smarting from the disappointment of losing his engine with just six laps remaining in the '73 race, ran away with the 1980 Daytona 500. Exactly a year later, it was '78

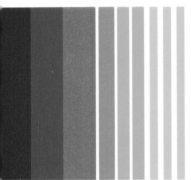

His seventh Daytona 500 was another new record for Richard Petty, but it raised the same old question: is it better to be good, or is it better to be lucky?

winner Bobby Allison who seemed poised on the threshold of victory. His Pontiac was the fastest qualifier, fastest in practice, fastest car, *period*. So when the green flag fell, no one was really surprised that Allison would lead nearly half of the 200 laps.

However, with just 26 laps remaining, the Ghost of Races Past appeared at the 1981 Daytona contest, and as it was during the 1970s the visit was another good news/bad news situation. The latter slapped Allison: the team miscalculated fuel mileage and his sputtering silver-and-black Le Mans had to coast, out of gas, half a lap back to the pits. Mr. Lucky inherited the lead, ducked in for a lightning-fast, splash-of-fuel-only pit stop, and motored home four seconds ahead of a visibly upset and utterly disappointed Bobby Allison.

His seventh Daytona 500 was another new record for Richard Petty, but it raised the same old question: is it better to be good, or is it better to be lucky? And NASCAR's version of the answer would simply be: it's best to be good, to be lucky, *and* to be the King.

1989 Daytona 500: Waltrip's Lucky 17

●●●●●●●●●●

The big question bouncing around the press tents and garages in the days leading up to the 1989 Daytona 500 had nothing to do with horsepower, aerodynamics, or radial tires. It was the 0-for-16 bull's-eye clearly visible on three-time NASCAR Cup Series champion Darrell Waltrip. Without actually saying it, there were a lot of people thinking it:

How will he lose *this* year's race?

There were black marks beside Waltrip's name for every previous attempt in the Great American Race. Bad cars, bad tires, bad decisions, bad crashes—you name the bad break, it found its way to, or back to, Waltrip. Sixteen years is a very long time to eat the same thing over and over again...especially if it's crow on the menu. The pressure, as it had every year since 1973, inched up just a little higher.

As the 1989 pre-500 Speedweeks festivities unfolded, two things were apparent: Chevrolet was the car to beat, and Ken Schrader had the fastest one on the track. When the checkered flag fell for the big race, he simply underlined what everyone already expected by leading 114 of the 200 laps. Dale Earnhardt was also armed with a very fast Monte Carlo but one hampered by a fuel flow problem. His car ran well in a draft but sputtered and coughed when it led, so he stayed safely tucked behind Schrader for most of the day.

Around Lap 165 Waltrip radioed his crew chief, Jeff Hammond, with a bold idea: since we can't outrun Schrader and Earnhardt, let's take a chance—a *huge* chance—and try to beat 'em on fuel mileage. Hammond immediately agreed to roll the dice. "We were running a half-second less than the leaders," he said. "Our calculations indicated we could go fifty laps easy, and we'd just have to squeeze out three or four more."

As the laps clicked off, Waltrip in the lead, Schrader and Earnhardt in frantic pursuit, the anxiety levels

Darrell Waltrip drives his Tide #17 car to victory against the Michael Waltrip #30 Country Time car during the Daytona 500 at the Daytona Speedway on February 19, 1989 at Daytona Beach, Florida.

climbed. "I thought I was out of gas a couple of times," Waltrip said. "I'd slosh the car around, get another ounce and go another hundred yards.

Hammond must have had two or three heart attacks. One time I yelled on the radio, 'That's it, Jeff, I'm out.' Then I yelled back, 'No, not yet, I'm still going.'

DAYTONA 500

We did that two or three times. It was wild."

But on this day, Waltrip's streak of Daytona luck changed. It was his 17th Daytona 500. His daughter, Jessica, was 17 months old on February 17. And his car number was 17. Waltrip took the checkered flag and celebrated by spiking his race helmet and performing an abbreviated version of the Icky Shuffle, the touchdown dance popularized by NFL rookie sensation Icky Woods, who led the Cincinnati Bengals that year to the "other" Super Bowl.

2002 Daytona 500: Marlin Bends the Rules

● ● ● ● ● ● ● ● ●

As the National Association for Stock Car Auto Racing ramped up the glittery high-profile preparations for the opening race of the 2002 season, it was very apparent how much the sport had evolved from its 1940s backroads roots. But million-dollar winners' shares, multimillion-dollar race teams, *mega-*million-dollar television contacts, and the high-tech racing machines couldn't completely obscure what the NASCAR press releases ignored. At the end of the day and the end of the race, it only mattered *who* was first across the finish line, not *how* you got there.

The sport originally blossomed when bootleggers in souped-up cars began racing each other to determine who was fastest. While that outlaw survivorism eventually had to bend to fair play, the rule-bending never entirely left the sport.

Ward Burton is given the checkered flag as he wins the 2002 Daytona 500 at the Daytona International Speedway in Daytona Beach, Florida, Sunday, February 17, 2002. In second is Elliott Sandler (21); third is Geoffrey Bodine (09); and fourth is Kurt Busch (97).

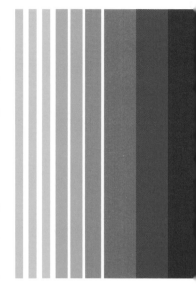

The sport originally blossomed when bootleggers in souped-up cars began racing each other to determine who was fastest. While that outlaw survivorism eventually had to bend to fair play, the rule-bending never entirely left the sport.

So while it may have been a surprise, it wasn't a complete shock to the people watching the 2002 Daytona 500—200,000 spectators and another 18.8 million tuned in to the race broadcast—when under the red flag Sterling Marlin dropped the driver's-side window net and hopped out of the Coors Light Dodge to bend his crumpled fender, and a rule or two.

When Mark Martin and Michael Waltrip tangled with five laps remaining, Marlin crunched his right front fender in a collision with race leader Jeff Gordon, but still beat Ward Burton's Caterpillar Dodge back to the start-finish line. NASCAR officials threw the red flag, which stopped the twenty-nine cars remaining on the track while the debris was cleared for a final three-lap shootout.

Item 10-5 of the 2002 NASCAR Cup Series rule-book is very clear: "Repairs or service of any nature will not be permitted when the race is halted due to a red flag." But knowing that his front tire would almost certainly explode due to friction from the fender rub, Marlin and crew chief Tony Glover decided to roll the dice and hope for the best. "I saw Earnhardt do it at Richmond one time in 1986, he got out and cleaned his windshield, so I thought it was okay," Marlin said.

There was a stunned silence, followed by a collective, "What is Sterling *doing?*" Which was of course followed by a swarm of on-track NASCAR officials, who informed the indignant Marlin he'd have to start at the end of the lead-lap cars.

Ward Burton inherited first place and beat Elliott Sadler, Geoff Bodine, and Kurt Busch to the finish line. "Today we had some luck," said Burton of his first Daytona 500 win. "We were just in the right place at the right time."

And Marlin? Instead of crashing with a flat tire, he was able to scramble back during the three-lap rush to finish in eighth place.

Janet Guthrie: The First Woman of the Great American Race
● ● ● ● ● ● ● ● ● ●

If it's possible to categorize as routine a race where forty-two competitors chase one another at 180 mph and bang fenders for 500 miles, then the 1977 Daytona 500 was pretty much as expected.

The previous season Cale Yarborough finished forty-second—dead last—at Daytona but a year later dominated the race. He managed to avoid the usual high-octane chicanery, survived a cut tire and a wild spin 'n' slide through the infield without losing so much as a fender or a lap, and won 1977's edition of the Great American Race. Richard Petty was Yarborough's only real challenger that day, but the engine in his Dodge blew up on Lap 111. Darrell Waltrip and David Pearson also had motors that went south before the checkered flag. Following Yarborough, the rest of the top five that day was Benny Parsons, Buddy Baker, Coo Coo Marlin, and Richard Brooks. Ricky Rudd finished twenty-second in his first Daytona 500 attempt.

But Rudd wasn't the highest-placing rookie.

That honor was earned with a twelfth-place finish by a thirty-eight-year-old driver with thirteen years of sports car road-racing experience, three Indianapolis 500 starts, a physics degree from the University of Michigan, a pilot's license, and enough on the ball to have made it through to the second round of NASA's Scientist-Astronaut program.

And one more bit of information about that twelfth-place driver: all but one year of their elementary education

Janet Guthrie at Daytona in 1977.

Gutherie holds her own at Daytona.

was completed at Miss Harris' Florida School for Girls.

Finishing twelfth that February afternoon in Daytona was Janet Guthrie, the first woman ever to drive in the Great American Race. She beat the odds—and a whole lot of her male competitors—on her way forward from the back of the pack. This accomplishment, in retrospect extraordinary by any-one's standards, irritated and upset some fellow competitors and fans, and rated maybe a single line in the Daytona 500 stories that appeared in newspapers around the country the following day. But race winner Yarborough, legendary for his toughness as a NASCAR competitor and usually even tougher to impress, was the first to stand up and salute Guthrie for her effort.

"She drives as well as any rookie I've seen. There is no question about her ability to race with us. More power to her. She has 'made it' in what I think is the most competitive racing circuit in the world."

2004 Daytona 500: Junior Wins!

• • • • • • • • •

In the two Daytona 500s following the tragic 2001 race that took the life of his father, Dale Earnhardt Jr. seemed to be building the same snakebitten résumé that kept the menacing number 3 Chevy—and Dale Sr.—out of Victory Lane for nineteen straight years.

In 2002, a blown tire damaged Junior's car and he finished thirty-sixth. The following year it was the alternator that went south, relegating him to twenty-ninth place. So heading into the 2004 season expectations for the number 8 team should have been somewhat realistic.

But it was Junior himself who raised eyebrows in the days leading up to the 500. First was a great run at the Rolex 24 at Daytona with co-drivers Tony Stewart and Andy Wallace in a sleek, stylish, and wickedly fast Crawford Chevrolet. A week later Earnhardt pushed Dale Jarrett to the Bud Shootout title, and then won a Gatorade Twin 125-mile qualifying race to put himself in the second row for the start of the Daytona 500. And when pole sitter Greg Biffle was moved to the back of the field because of an engine change, NASCAR's favorite son was suddenly starting on the front row.

After the green flag finally waved on that sunny Sunday afternoon, Junior was off like a shot and leading the race before the end of the first lap. He stayed there for the next 29 and was up front three other times during the first 250 miles. And when he wasn't leading it was Earnhardt's pal Tony Stewart in charge; together they were a dominating combination.

"Everybody tried to separate Dale and me," Stewart said. "But our plan was to get together and run together."

The duo stayed in or near the front until green-flag pit stops on Lap 169 shuffled the field, but it only took Stewart six trips around to regain the lead. And just six laps after that, Junior made the final pass of the day and raced to the checkered flag to claim his first Daytona 500. "Trust me, I did everything I could to win this race," Stewart said afterwards. "He outdrove us and beat us, plain and simple."

"Good God, I'm the Daytona 500 champion!" an elated Dale Jr. screamed during the Victory Lane celebration, and the 200,000 wildly cheering fans thoroughly enjoyed a NASCAR family–style win. But besides the victory, and the honor of joining the Pettys and Allisons on the father-son Daytona 500 winner's pedestal, Junior told the assembled media he was able to share an even greater thrill with the Intimidator during the closing laps of the race.

"My dad was in the passenger seat right with me today. And I am sure he had a blast."

Dale Earnhardt Jr., driver of #8 Chevy, celebrates with his crew at the finish line after winning the Daytona 500, Sunday, February 15, 2004 at Daytona International Speedway in Daytona Beach, Florida.

*He was tenacious. He was fearsome. He was
seat-of-the-pants, white-knuckle racing at its finest. And following
his dogfight at The Winston in Charlotte on May 17, 1987,
Dale Earnhardt would forever be known as "The Intimidator."*

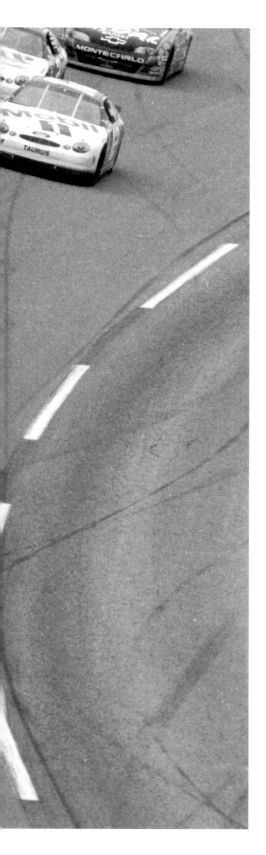

Daytona 500 Victory: Twenty Years in the Making

●●●●●●●●●

Call them the unlucky. The star-crossed. The big names without the big games. For the hapless Boston Red Sox, it was the World Series. For Ivan Lendl, Wimbledon. Dan Marino and John Elway, the Super Bowl.

And for Dale Earnhardt, it was the Daytona 500.

Every February for two disheartening decades, one of NASCAR's most

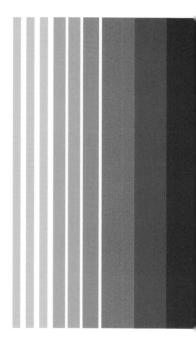

Every February for two disheartening decades, one of NASCAR's most renowned drivers, a man who'd conquered just about every major race there was to win, rode into Daytona to claim the holy grail of the NASCAR Cup series. Nineteen times he'd faced down the Great American Race. Nineteen times he'd trudged home empty-handed, a beaten man.

renowned drivers, a man who'd conquered just about every major race there was to win, rode into Daytona to claim the holy grail of the NASCAR Cup Series. Nineteen times he'd faced down the Great American Race. Nineteen times he'd trudged home empty-handed, a beaten man.

"It was unbelievable," race analyst Benny Parsons said. "If you had written the story of Dale and the Daytona 500 and taken it to Hollywood, they would have laughed you out of town and said, 'Get out of here! No one has this much bad luck!'"

Dale Earnhardt takes the checkered flag he chased for over twenty years.

Earnhardt's Daytona tribulations made Job look fortunate. There were blown leads, unexpected break-downs, last-minute heroics that fell nanoseconds short. Not once but twice he'd been edged out on the final lap. He'd blown a tire a breath away from the checkered flag. He had run out of gas, flipped his car, blew an engine, all with the brass ring tickling his fingertips.

"I've won a lot of Daytona 499s," the perennial bridesmaid once quipped.

But it was no joke. It burned him up. And he knew that for all his big-time wins, his record seven Cup championships, his untold millions in earnings, and the

admiration of legions of fans, his career would never be legit until he landed the big kahuna. It was that simple.

Few thought 1998 would be his year. At forty-six, Earnhardt was coming off one of the most disappointing seasons of his career and was riding a fifty-nine-race winless streak that stretched back to

March 1996. He'd never seen a slump like this. But he surely cocked an eyebrow when a month earlier his bad-luck brother John Elway managed to bag his own white whale after fifteen years of heartbreak.

"If Elway can win a Super Bowl," Earnhardt declared before climbing into his legendary black number 3 Chevy for attempt number twenty on February 15, "I can win the Daytona 500." He rubbed the lucky penny he'd glued to the dashboard, strapped in, and prepared to exorcise his demons.

Gunning the brand-new engine, he jumped out to an early lead and held on for 34 laps. Overtaken by Daytona's defending champ, Jeff Gordon, Earnhardt fell a full ten cars off the pace, but in classic Intimidator style managed to hammer and draft his way back through the crowded field. In six laps he'd made up five spots and was soon tailing the lead pack, stalking Gordon.

By Lap 121 of the 200-lap contest, the hunter caught his prey, and he and Gordon, yoked together like drafthorses, blistered down the backstretch until the number 24 Chevy nailed a chunk of debris and mangled his front air-dam. Bad luck. Earnhardt blew by him to retake the point. A determined Rusty Wallace then barreled in to challenge, but the Intimidator received a helpful bump from teammate Mike Skinner that sent him into the clear with just 23 laps to go. The crowd of 175,000 held its breath and waited for the wrath of God.

Yet somehow the wheels stayed on and the engine continued to turn. With the field stacked three-wide and knocking the tar out of each other in his rearview, Earnhardt stormed toward the final lap. And then a collision—one that remarkably didn't involve the number 3 car—brought out the caution, preserving his lead. It was over. Ralph Dale Earnhardt Sr. had won the Daytona 500.

"I'll admit it," the quintessential tough guy conceded, "my eyes watered up coming to take the checkered....That's one of the greatest feelings in your life, to work that many years and come so close and be so dominant and finally win that race."

Friends and foes alike gather along pit road to congratulate the Intimidator for his Daytona 500 win.

The scene as Earnhardt rolled toward Victory Lane was pure magic, as virtually every member of every team, joined by the longtime racing press, thronged onto pit road to mob him with congratulatory handshakes and high-fives and heartfelt slaps to the roof of the number 3 car. It no longer mattered that the old outlaw had wrecked them at Bristol or spun them at Talladega or cussed them silly in the garage at Darlington. For that moment, he was everybody's champ, and even the "Anybody but Earnhardt" brigade

Dale Earnhardt and crew celebrate his 1998 victory in the Daytona 500.

in the grandstands couldn't help cracking a smile.

"It's kinda neat," said longtime on-track nemesis Rusty Wallace, who once remarked semi-seriously that the Intimidator would down his own mother to win. "As much as he's meant to the sport, he deserves it."

"We all loved for him to be there [in Victory Lane]," Jeff Gordon told reporters. "He's earned it, man."

After a quick detour to the infield grass to carve out a "3" with a series of wild donuts, Earnhardt entered the winner's circle to a raucous cheer. And if anybody had forgotten why he was NASCAR's signature personality, he made it clear when he bounded onto the podium for his victory interview.

"I'm here! And I've got that monkey off my back!" he bellowed, hurling a filthy stuffed gorilla at the press corps, his steel-eyed glare softening into a rakish smile beneath the gunslinger's mustache. Suddenly, he was a cocky rookie again, strutting and preening and promising an eighth championship by the end of the year. And just as suddenly, he turned philosophical.

"I wrote the book here," he said, recalling his years of disappointment, all the close calls, the near misses and frustrations. "This is the last chapter. We'll start a new book now."

Sadly, that new volume would be far too short. Just three years and three days later, on the very same spot where he'd notched the most important victory of his life, forty-nine-year-old Dale Earnhardt would be killed after smacking the wall head-on going into the final lap of the Daytona 500.

Transformed from Intimidator to icon, the legend of Dale Earnhardt still looms larger than life, and like so many battles in his storied career, the memory of his Daytona 500 victory lives on.

Dale Rides the Air at Talladega

• • • • • • • • •

"**D**ale could will his car to do whatever the hell he wanted it to do," crew chief Andy Petree once said of the Intimidator. He'd seen it. The miraculous rallies. The prodigious passes. The mysterious bursts of speed through holes that didn't exist.

And when it came to high-speed drafting, the Man in Black became the Prince of Darkness.

"This man could see the air," a stupefied Dale Jarrett once said. "He denied it, but I saw him do things that proved it." And what he did at the Winston 500 at Talladega on October 15, 2000, still has people scratching their heads in wonder.

That weekend began on a sour note for Earnhardt with the eleventh-hour introduction of even more restrictive restrictor plates, horsepower-sapping devices designed to curb "unsafe" speeds on big tracks like Talladega and Daytona.

Ever the lone wolf, Earnhardt detested the bunched-up, pack-style racing they engendered, although he'd virtually written the book on the art.

Disgusted with the wet-blanket move, he traipsed back to the garage clutching the modified device in front of him like a sack of dog waste.

The next afternoon, running early in a nose-to-tail conga line on the 2.66-mile tri-oval, he discovered that NASCAR's changes had drastically altered the track's drafting dynamics.

A driver could search the whole race and not find the right groove, and Earnhardt spent much of the afternoon doing just that. High, low, front, back—nothing seemed to work. But his brain was spinning

Dale Earnhardt (3) of Kannapolis, N.C., leads Mike Skinner (31) of Susanville, California and Dale Earnhardt Jr (8) of Kannapolis, North Carolina, during the Winston 500 on Sunday afternoon, October 15, 2000, at the Talladega Superspeedway in Talladega, Alabama. Earnhardt won the race.

furiously, calculating the possibilities.

Boxed in and running eighteenth with just five laps remaining, it seemed his bag of tricks was dry. And then it happened. He gave Rich Bickle a nudge high and moved by him. Four laps to go. On the backstretch, he discovered a tunnel and blew by six more cars. Then

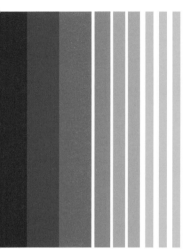

Earnhardt weaved to break the draft and held off the jackals for his 10th career win at Talladega, as 140,000 delirious fans rubbed their eyes in amazement. Was it possible? Was he even human?

another. With three laps left, he was eighth. He scuttled to the outside, then the middle, then back again, riding the draft. Competitors dropped. Earnhardt was fourth.

"The Intimidator is scraped and beaten...but he will not be denied!" shouted ESPN broadcaster Jerry Punch. "Two laps to go...Wow!"

Heading into the finale, they were running three-wide at the point, with Earnhardt on the outside. Kenny Wallace, hanging on Earnhardt's backside with Joe Nemechek inches behind, popped the Intimidator, sending their three-car draft line flying past the others. And then there was no getting around the number 3 car.

Earnhardt weaved to break the draft and held off the jackals for his tenth career win at Talladega, as 140,000 delirious fans rubbed their eyes in amazement. Was it possible? Was he even human?

"He's behind me and he still wins?" asked a befuddled Jeff Gordon, who finished fourth. "My gosh, are you kidding me?"

The jubilant forty-eight-year-old Earnhardt, in serious contention for a championship for the first time since 1995, hopped from his car and danced a jig in front of the press box. "They need to work out, don't they?" he wisecracked of his competitors. "I'm not a bit tired."

Later, before retiring to his trailer for a celebratory vodka-and-Sunny Delight, he marveled at his accomplishment. "It's beyond me," he confessed. "You saw it. I couldn't believe it."

The astonishing victory—his seventy-sixth in a career of mind-boggling wins—would be his last.

"The Intimidator" Is Born
• • • • • • • • •

He was tenacious. He was fearsome. He was seat-of-the-pants, white-knuckle racing at its finest. And following his dogfight at The Winston in Charlotte on May 17, 1987, Dale Earnhardt would forever be known as "the Intimidator."

"That's about the nearest thing you can get to good old grassroots racing," Rusty Wallace remarked of the rowdy showdown, which featured a hefty dose of metal-scraping, a fistfight or two, and enough trash talk to rival professional wrestling. "Earnhardt drove like an absolute madman."

A madman piloting a 700-horsepower lawn mower.

The mayhem began during the $200,000 competition's final portion, a ten-lap shootout that saw Earnhardt and Bill Elliott go toe-to-toe from the opening bell. Just seconds into the race, pole sitter Elliott, pinched to the apron by Earnhardt and Geoff Bodine, clipped Bodine, allowing Earnhardt, who started fourth, to squeeze by on the inside for the lead. Elliott fell in behind, taking a few neighborly whacks at the number 3 car's bumper.

Then, with seven laps left, it got vicious. Coming out of Turn 4, the rivals exchanged paint, and Elliott sent Earnhardt careening off the track and into the infield grass. A mere mortal would have lost control and watched ruefully as the field whizzed by. But Earnhardt mashed the accelerator, rocketing down

the lawn at 170 mph before regaining the track fifty yards later...*ahead of Elliott*. The grandstands went berserk.

The plow through the pasture didn't end it. Elliott had payback coming. A lap later, with the culprit on his outside, Earnhardt squeezed him to the wall. Elliott's left rear fender crumpled, cutting a tire. Earnhardt then chased down Terry Labonte, who'd snaked ahead while Dale was dispensing his unique brand of automotive justice, to take the win by 0.74 seconds.

It was a breathtaking display of dominance, but Elliott wasn't impressed. He roadblocked Earnhardt on the cool-down lap. Words were exchanged. Crew members pounded their knuckles. Near the pits, Kyle Petty and Rusty Wallace began trading wallops over the finer points of sportsmanship. The entire garage seemed primed to explode. But Earnhardt and Elliott managed to settle things like gentlemen, with threats and finger-pointing.

"If a man has to run over you to beat you, it's time to stop," Elliott fumed. "I'm sick of it. Everyone knows his style. If somebody doesn't do something about this, we're coming back next week and we'll see what happens."

Earnhardt didn't sweat the bounty on his head and in typical fashion issued a bare-knuckle challenge of his own. "Elliott put me in the grass and that upset me," he said. "It's all over now, as far as I'm concerned. But if Bill still wants to do something about it, I'll stand flat-footed with him any day."

Earnhardt would finish 1987 by taking the points championship for the second straight year, notching a career-high eleven victories. But his legendary "Pass in the Grass" performance would outshine them all, standing as a testament to the unparalleled skill and tough-as-nails attitude that made him the Intimidator.

Earnhardt Ties the King in Cup Titles
• • • • • • • • • •

It took NASCAR's most revered driver, Richard Petty, twenty years to establish a record most thought could never be matched. It took Dale Earnhardt just fifteen to make them think again.

Between 1980 and 1993, Earnhardt amassed a jaw-dropping six championships—'80, '86, '87, '90, '91, and '93, more than all his active competitors combined—and was already being lionized as one of racing's all-time greats. By the fall of 1994, leading once again in the points race and needing just one more title to catch Petty, the Intimidator seemed poised to join the King at royal court.

For the high school dropout who never imagined he'd win a single championship, let alone seven, his days sweating in the textile mills of Kannapolis, racing dirt tracks for rent money, and hightailing it from angry creditors must have seemed light-years away.

And so was his competition. Heading into Rockingham for the twenty-ninth race of the season on October 23, 1994, Earnhardt was so far ahead of second-place Rusty Wallace that all he needed to do to reach the record books was lay back and place twenty-eighth or better in the final three contests.

Right, and Secretariat could have loped to

victory in the Triple Crown.

In front of a packed house at North Carolina Motor Speedway, the forty-three-year-old master put on a clinic, showcasing all the competitiveness, grit, and pure driving skill that had brought him to the brink of NASCAR immortality.

Starting twentieth, he worked his way forward, diving into turns and blasting down straightaways, to lead by Lap 173. He'd fallen back during the middle stretch, but with 77 laps to go, he'd take the point again, slingshotting past Rick Mast. Mast's number 1 Ford clearly had the speed over Earnhardt's Chevy, but dog the master as he might, Mast, like so many frustrated competitors before him, couldn't find his way around the number 3 car. "Earnhardt's bumper gets mighty wide there at the end," he'd lament.

The shootout ended with Earnhardt taking the checkered flag just 0.06 seconds ahead of Mast for his

Dale Earnhardt celebrates with his Winston Cup Series Trophy after winning the AC Delco 500 and sealing the title at the North Carolina Motor Speedway in Rockingham, North Carolina.

fourth win of the season and clinching the championship two races ahead of schedule. He was in seventh heaven.

At the post-race press conference, an emotional Earnhardt dedicated the title to his old buddy Neil Bonnett, killed earlier that year during a practice run at Daytona, and then paid homage to the army of old-school vets whose noses he'd tweaked as a young ruffian filled with piss and vinegar.

"A lot of folks have helped me get where I am," he told the crowd. "The Pearsons, Pettys, Jarretts, Allisons, and Yarboroughs—they were aggressive racers and that's the way I drive. They made me a better racer.

"But Richard Petty is still the King and he'll always be the King. I'm a seven-time champion."

Years earlier, Petty himself had weighed in on Earnhardt's future in the sport.

"When you saw [Dale] coming, you braced yourself," he said. "You knew that if he didn't calm down, he wasn't going to make it. But you also knew that if he ever got all that talent and attitude harnessed, he was going to be pretty darn good."

Just how good, not even the King could have imagined.

The Intimidator Returns

● ● ● ● ● ● ● ● ●

For sheer audacity, it would be difficult to beat Dale Earnhardt's no-holds-barred, wrecking-ball assault at the 1995 Goody's 500 at Bristol Motor Speedway on August 28, 1999. But leave it to the Man in Black to top himself. Four years after his infamous "smack in the back" propelled Terry Labonte sideways across the finish line at the storied half-mile oval, Earnhardt would provide the Bristol crowd with an even more memorable final-lap fiasco. And this time,

Dale Earnhardt of Kannapolis, North Carolina, celebrates his win in the Goody's 500 in Bristol, Tennessee, Saturday, August 28, 1999.

Labonte wouldn't be smiling.

Earnhardt entered 1999 coming off a couple unremarkable seasons, by his standards. While he'd finished in the top ten in points in both '97 and '98, he'd notched just a single win in sixty-five races, a far cry from his twenty-four victories and four Winston Cup championships in the first half of the decade. At forty-eight, perhaps time was catching up with him. After all, even his youngest son, twenty-four-year-old Dale Jr., had now joined the slew of NASCAR fledglings trying to run him down.

But Old Ironhead was showing flashes of his earlier brilliance. He'd finished in the top ten in fourteen of twenty-three races. He was feeling strong. And like a veteran heavyweight, he was itching to demonstrate that his wicked knockout punch hadn't deserted him. And so the curtain rose on Bristol.

Under a full moon, 140,000 fans watched rapt as Earnhardt and Terry Labonte exchanged the lead four times over the last 121 laps. The duel turned fiery with just two laps to go, as Labonte, after pitting for fresh tires, roared back from fifth place and edged up beside Earnhardt going into the third turn. The two bumped as Labonte fought for the point on the outside. In Turn 4 they scraped paint again, and this time Labonte shot onto the frontstretch with the lead.

But if Earnhardt's rhubarb years on the South's short tracks had taught him anything, it was this: nobody steals your victory without a price. The gloves came off. With less than a yard separating the two heading into the final lap, Earnhardt went low into the first turn and caught Labonte's bumper. A plume of white smoke exploded from the number 5 car's tires and Labonte went spinning through traffic down the backstretch, spewing profanities into his radio as he met the wall. Game, set, match.

Drowning the cheers, a chorus of boos and middle-finger salutes met Earnhardt as he crossed the finish line for his seventy-third career victory. With corks popping, the grinning champ defended his move. "I didn't mean to wreck him," he said. "I just wanted to rattle his cage a bit. But I bumped him too hard and turned him loose."

The apology didn't sway many. "There are some guys that will race you clean," said Ricky Rudd, who finished third. "The guy that spun Terry is not one of those guys. But you've got to think of that when you pass him. You can't give him that free shot."

Indeed. The hard-nosed bad boy of NASCAR hadn't built his reputation over twenty years by donning kid gloves and making nice, and he certainly wasn't about to soften with age. "This is racing," he was fond of saying. "It ain't tennis." The Intimidator was back.

The Dogfight at Bristol

· · · · · · · · · ·

The cramped half-mile oval at Bristol has always been a stock car gladiator's dream. With way too much horsepower in way too small a space, the track seems tailor-made for crowd-pleasing destruction. Hot tempers, busted fenders—it was everything Dale Earnhardt lived for. Sprinkle a few August showers on the concrete, and voilà, you get one of the greatest knock-down, drag-out battles of the Intimidator's career and one of NASCAR's wildest finishes.

Just three weeks after his historic win at the

Brickyard put the public on notice that he was still in the points race, Earnhardt sent a stern message to his competitors: get in my way and I'll run right through you. A mere 32 laps into the soggy Goody's 500 on August 26, 1995, the Man in Black made good on that promise, swapping chrome with Rusty Wallace as the two battled for fourth place and spinning Wallace's number 2 Ford into the wall on the straightaway. A furious Wallace bumped Earnhardt during the ensuing caution, and race officials banished the Intimidator to the back of the class for playing too rough.

The neighborhood bully wouldn't be denied. He relentlessly muscled his way to the front again before being clipped. And then again. And again. Collisions, slow pits—it didn't seem to matter; each time Earnhardt fell behind, he'd cut a new swath of destruction through the field and his battered black machine would be back again, breathing menacingly down the leader's rear bumper.

The final charge came with 70 laps to go. Stuck in ninth position, Earnhardt worked his way up to sixth by Lap 472. Fifteen more and he was in second, a quarter-lap behind front-runner Terry Labonte, who appeared to have enough room to coast to a comfortable win. "I really didn't think he had enough laps to catch us," Labonte said. "Then I got caught."

Heading into the last lap, Labonte was forced to brake behind a herd of lapped cars. Sensing the drama, Bristol's record crowd of 79,000 rose to its feet. Here came Earnhardt, flying into the final turn, just behind the logjam. And then, POW! Earnhardt plowed into the back of Labonte's number 5 Chevy, which slammed off Greg Sacks's car, but still slid sideways over the finish line for the win. Labonte then careened head-on into the outside wall, coming to rest with the front end nearly in the driver's seat and the back a pile of crushed metal. Earnhardt took second.

With the spectacular 500-lap dogfight in the books, it seemed inevitable that tempers would boil over. But the post-race fireworks didn't come from Labonte, who took the whole episode in stride ("I don't ever remember going across the finish line sideways for a

win," he joked), but from Rusty Wallace, who was still fuming over his early on-track run-in with Earnhardt.

As Earnhardt spoke with reporters, Wallace approached and hurled a water bottle, which grazed Earnhardt's head. "You better watch that [expletive] bumper," Wallace growled. Bystanders quickly stepped between the two men. "I ain't forgetting this," Wallace shouted. "Yours is coming." The Intimidator just smirked at his adversary and winked. "Hey, don't forget nothing," he drawled.

Earnhardt and Gordon Battle at the Brickyard

● ● ● ● ● ● ● ● ●

Heading into the 1995 season, the Man in Black seemed invincible. He'd just captured his record-tying seventh Cup championship—his fourth in five years—joining Richard Petty atop the pantheon of NASCAR's all-time greats. Now, at age forty-four, he was the odds-on favorite to topple the King's mark by winning an eighth.

But a young competitor was thumping on his fender. At twenty-three, fresh-faced Jeff Gordon had taken Rookie of the Year honors in 1993 and racked up fourteen Top 10 finishes in 1994, including a major win in the first-ever Indianapolis Brickyard 400. The talk around the garage was that this could be the year the kid pried the pistol from the grizzled warrior's hands.

The Intimidator was having none of it. He hit 1995 like a bat out of hell, placing in the top five in six out of seven races, with a win and three second-place finishes. But a series of midseason setbacks took their toll. By the time NASCAR rolled into Indianapolis on August 5, the champ had slipped from first to a distant third in the standings and Gordon was beginning to pull away. With twelve races left, and one of racing's most prestigious contests staring him in the face, Earnhardt needed to make a statement.

He didn't disappoint. Following a four-hour rain

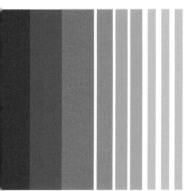

The win was the biggest and richest of Earnhardt's career, but he seemed less interested in celebrating than putting the doubters in their place.

delay, Indy's 325,000 waterlogged fans were treated to a dandy 160-lap battle. In a replay of 1994, Earnhardt brushed the wall early but maintained control, as Gordon jumped out to a quick lead from the pole. Earnhardt would later joke that the damage to his right front fender made his car faster, but he seemed content to hang back for much of the afternoon while the lead changed hands some sixteen times.

With about 65 laps remaining, the Intimidator began to move, and by the time leader Rusty Wallace was held up by a pit-road jam on Lap 130, Earnhardt had the momentum to blast by him on the backstretch. After a hard-charging Jeff Burton got too chummy with the number 3 car and spun, bringing out the race's only caution, it was clean air for Earnhardt, who stubbornly held off Wallace and Dale Jarrett

for the final 28 laps to take the checkered by just 0.37 seconds. Gordon, plagued by handling problems, finished sixth.

The win was the biggest and richest of Earnhardt's career, but he seemed less interested in celebrating than putting the doubters in their place.

When a reporter asked how it felt to creep out of Gordon's shadow with a huge victory, Earnhardt removed his ever-present shades and glowered. "Do you think I needed to reestablish myself? Do you think people have just completely forgot about me? Just because a Jeff Gordon gets ahead of us in points doesn't mean we're through. We're not dead yet."

With those words, and a few well-aimed barbs at Gordon, Earnhardt began a tenacious climb back into contention. He'd make it closer than anyone expected, finishing in the top three in seven of the last ten races and falling just 34 points shy of a record-setting eighth title.

Defiant in defeat, Earnhardt continued to haze the youngster he'd derisively dubbed Wonder Boy. Months after the season, he still crowed about being "the only man to have ever won the Brickyard 400."

From Rookie of the Year to Cup Champion

● ● ● ● ● ● ● ● ● ●

The young Dale Earnhardt was a Hank Williams song come to life, a raucous good ol' boy who scraped and scrapped, raised plenty of hell, and wasn't afraid to bust his knuckles to get what he wanted—on or off the track.

He may have been born into NASCAR royalty, but there was no silver platter. By the time he was twenty-five, the high school dropout had burned through two marriages, fathered three kids, and careened around enough minor-league dirt tracks to make a carousel dizzy. Bouncing from one thankless job to another—mechanic, mill worker, welder—and buried $11,000 deep in debt, he never gave up his dream of one day competing in the Cup Series.

And then the call came. In 1979 he was offered his first full-season ride by owner Rod Osterlund, and the twenty-eight-year-old from Kannapolis, North

Dale Earnhardt holds aloft a dummy front page proclaiming him the 1980 NASCAR Grand National Champion at the Los Angeles Times 500, November 15, 1980.

Carolina, stunned everyone by posting seventeen Top 10 finishes in twenty-seven starts, coming in seventh in points and garnering NASCAR Rookie of the Year honors.

But the taste of triumph only whetted his appetite. "That ain't s——t," he reportedly told friends after the 1979 season. "Next year I'm gonna be Winston Cup points champion." It was a bold boast, considering no sophomore had come close to winning a title in NASCAR's thirty-one-year history. Earnhardt didn't care.

He greeted 1980 with a non-points victory and immediately raised the hackles of racing's elite with his brazenness. "There might be a trick or two that Richard Petty and Bobby Allison haven't shown me yet," he boasted, "but I know I'm as good as they are."

"Earnhardt has more damn nerve than a sore tooth," veteran Buddy Baker complained of the young swaggerer. He wasn't alone. But the kid had the chops to back it up. He started the year by reeling off six straight Top 5 finishes, including two wins—one after starting light-years away, in thirty-first position—and never looked back.

The old warriors Petty and Yarborough snapped at the upstart's heels from the season's get-go. But Earnhardt, who took the points lead with a fourth-place finish at the Daytona 500 and never relinquished it, was able to pad his margin with two hard-charging late-season victories at Martinsville and Charlotte. When the year's final checkered fell at California's Ontario Speedway on November 15, 1980, NASCAR crowned its brand-new champion.

Earnhardt's astonishing five victories and twenty-four Top 10 finishes (including nineteen in the top five) dispelled any notion that he was just a flash in the pan. And his old-school, paint-swapping style, fighting tooth and nail for every pass, in every corner and down every straightaway, quickly won admirers in the grandstands, and enemies on the track.

By the time the leather-faced, mustachioed newcomer waltzed into NASCAR's year-end winner's banquet in his cowboy boots, a star had been born, and a legion of hardscrabble, blue-collar fans had found themselves a new honky-tonk hero.

The Man in Black/ The Man of Steel

• • • • • • • • •

"Earnhardt has always had the ability to intimidate," Humpy Wheeler, president of Lowe's Speedway, once remarked. "People just don't like to see that black car on their bumper."

And God help the thickheaded fool who refused to open up when that car came knocking—there'd be hell to pay, in Bondo and sheet metal. "I would hate to have me behind me," confessed Earnhardt, who'd put his stamp on more fenders than GM.

But sooner or later, many imagined, the chickens would come home to roost. And then they'd see what the man was made of.

That moment came on July 28, 1996. And it nearly ended the forty-five-year-old Earnhardt's life. Leading the DieHard 500 at Talladega, the Intimidator roared into Turn 1 of Lap 117 with Sterling Marlin riding his right rear and Ernie Irvan inches from his bumper. The frustrated Irvan tagged the number 4 car, which then hit Earnhardt, sending him into the wall.

At 190 mph, the impact crushed Earnhardt's sternum like an eggshell, and his car flipped down the frontstretch like a 3,400-pound Ping-Pong ball. Derrike Cope nailed it, snapping Earnhardt's collarbone and bruising his pelvis. The mangled hulk slid on its side into traffic. Robert Pressley plowed into the roof, crushing it to within six inches of the gearshift. The car lurched and flipped upright, facing traffic. Kenny Schrader cracked it head-on.

Earnhardt, crawling from the wreck, fell to his knees. The pain was excruciating, but he refused a stretcher, gave the thumbs-up to the crowd, and somehow managed to walk to a waiting ambulance.

When news came down that Earnhardt would race in the Brickyard 400 six days later, few could believe it. But there he was, behind the wheel of the number 3 car, taped together like a rag doll and running at 170 mph before the pain became so unbearable that he handed the reins to alternate Mike Skinner. It was the toughest decision of his life. "It was hard to get out of there," he told the press, wincing, his eyes welling up with tears. "This is my life right here."

It wouldn't happen again. Against the advice of his doctors, his team owner, his friends, his family, and NASCAR president Bill France Jr., the mule-stubborn Ironhead, still in agony, raced again one week later at Watkins Glen, breaking the track qualifying record and rolling to a sixth-place finish on the eleven-turn road course. Everyone gulped at his fortitude.

"[Earnhardt] is the man," Jeff Gordon's crew chief, Ray Evernham, said after that race. "Until you can do what he does, you're second. That's it. The rest of us, as far as I'm concerned, are wannabes."

Still healing from his horrendous injuries, he proved he was the hardest of the hardcore by running every one of the remaining eleven races that season in constant pain, finishing in the top ten four times and fourth in overall points.

"I guess it's just my ego," Earnhardt said of his courageous run. "That's the bottom line."

A First for the Number 3

● ● ● ● ● ● ● ● ●

When Dale Earnhardt, fresh off his first Cup championship, suddenly found himself adrift without a ride in 1981, it was his hunting buddy and fellow driver Richard Childress who threw out the life preserver. Childress, who had run 285 races over a dozen years without a win, had read the writing on the wall. If he wanted success in NASCAR, he'd have to climb out of the driver's seat and pitch the keys to someone else.

"It was the toughest thing I ever had to do," Childress said. "But I knew Dale was one of the best raw talents that had come along in a long time, so I got out."

Their initial partnership lasted only a single season. They attracted no sponsors. They posted no wins. At year's end, Childress glumly suggested over a six-pack that Earnhardt find himself a better team. Resignedly, the thirty-year-old champ departed for greener pastures with owner Bud Moore. But Childress's magnanimity had made an indelible impression.

"Nobody might have ever given me another shot," Earnhardt remembered years later. "I might have been back on the short tracks and back working in a textile mill somewhere. He saved my butt. And I never forgot that."

So when Childress managed to land a lucrative contract with Wrangler Jeans for the 1984 season, the loyal Earnhardt repaid the favor and hopped behind the wheel.

The team clicked instantly. After eighteen races, they led the points standings and had fifteen top ten finishes. But by late summer they were still searching for that first victory.

It came at Talladega on July 29, 1984. In a

Dale Earnhardt leads the field into the third turn at Talladega during a 1984 event.

heady battle marked by sixty-eight lead changes, ten blown engines, and a slew of spectacular crashes, Earnhardt managed to survive and steer himself into striking position on the final go-round. With fifteen cars in the lead lap and Terry Labonte out front, Earnhardt made his move on the backstretch, barreling into the point and holding off Labonte

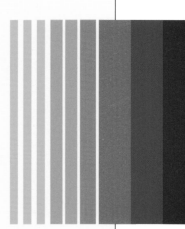

At year's end, Childress glumly suggested over a six-pack that Earnhardt find himself a better team. Resignedly, the 30-year-old champ departed for greener pastures with owner Bud Moore.

and Buddy Baker through the final two turns. As he shot across the finish line for his first ever win in the number 3 car, he waved jubilantly to the crowd.

The Earnhardt-Childress team would falter in the last third of the season, winning just once more, in Atlanta, and dropping to fourth in the final standings. But the seed had been planted, and over the next sixteen years that victory at Talladega would blossom into one of the greatest success stories in NASCAR history.

Years later, Childress, musing on the sixty-seven victories and six Cup championships he and Earnhardt had claimed during their illustrious ride, could still recall the night in 1981 when they'd met at the Downtowner Inn in Alabama to ink the new partnership. "I'd say it worked out," he joked. "Wouldn't you?"

Chapter Nine

ONE-WIN WONDERS

After taking the lead with less than 30 laps left in the 200-lap contest, Wendell Scott put some distance between himself and the front pack, which included Ned Jarrett, Richard Petty, and Buck Baker.

Wendell Scott: The First African American Driver to Win at NASCAR's Top Level

●●●●●●●●●●

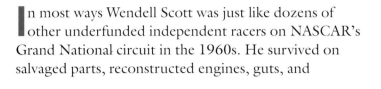

In most ways Wendell Scott was just like dozens of other underfunded independent racers on NASCAR's Grand National circuit in the 1960s. He survived on salvaged parts, reconstructed engines, guts, and ingenuity while endlessly scraping the bottom of the barrel for a few nickels to keep his dream alive.

But two things set him apart. First, he was better than most other drivers. Second, Wendell Scott was black.

And in a sport with roots sunk deep in the white working-class culture of the South, the wrong skin color could still be a serious detriment. While Jesse Owens and Jackie Robinson may have broken the athletic color barrier a generation earlier, NASCAR fans weren't about to tear down the Stars 'n' Bars and raise the banner of racial brotherhood.

"Back in those days," one NASCAR official said, "people could be very ugly when it came to race."

That ugliness reared its head at nearly every track Scott and his wife and six kids visited. There were racial taunts and flying garbage. There was on-track subterfuge and sabotage in the garage. There were even death threats from the Klan.

"If I'd have went through what Wendell Scott went through, I'd have never made it," said driver Junior Johnson. "And if I had to race the stuff he had, I wouldn't have lasted ten races. His determination was a thousand times more than what mine was."

That determination kept Scott running in NASCAR's Grand National (now Cup Series) Division for more than a dozen years, during which he competed in 495 races and logged 147 top ten finishes. For nine straight seasons he finished twentieth or better in points, including a four-season streak (1966–69) in the top ten, when he regularly edged out NASCAR legends like Ned Jarrett, Buddy Baker, Bobby Allison, and Cale Yarborough.

A former bootlegger from Danville,

Wendell Scott working on his car.

Virginia, Scott got his start as the result of a jailhouse bargain. While detained on charges of whiskey-running, he was approached by a local race promoter with a devious offer of posting bail if Scott would run at his track that evening.

It didn't take a lot of arm-twisting. The champion bootlegger quickly became a champion dirt-track racer, and over the next decade he dominated the Dixie circuit, winning more than 120 races and claiming NASCAR's 1959 Virginia State Sportsman title. In 1961 Scott made the jump to NASCAR's top-level Grand National Division.

Surviving in the Grand Nationals was a constant struggle for Scott, both economically and socially, but he made it work despite the indignities and isolation he suffered.

"He overcame many hurdles," said Scott's son Franklin, who spent his teenage years traveling with the family to races and working with his brothers on his father's pit crew. "But he never let it faze him to the point where it made him hostile."

That was true most of the time. But Scott wasn't above flexing some muscle if his antagonists pushed it too far. If that meant threatening to punch Bobby Allison in the nose for spinning him or leveling a pistol

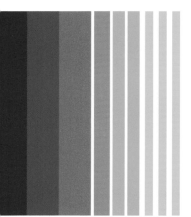

"He probably did more with less than any driver I've ever seen," said racer Ned Jarrett. "But he just never really got the [financial] break he needed to show the talents that he had ...

at a bullying Jack Smith in the middle of a race, so be it. A man has a right to protect his livelihood, especially when he's walking a constant tightrope between penury and the poorhouse and has seven hungry mouths to feed.

On December 1, 1963, Scott would roll his meal ticket onto the half-mile dirt track at Jacksonville Speedway Park. In less than two hours, he would be involved in one of the most controversial decisions in NASCAR history.

After taking the lead with less than 30 laps left in the 200-lap contest, Scott put some distance between himself and the front pack, which included Ned Jarrett, Richard Petty, and Buck Baker, who was running second. Over the next few laps that margin would grow as Scott put the hammer down. By the time he entered the final turn, he had lapped the field twice, but there was no checkered flag waiting for him at the finish line.

Scott completed another lap. Still no checkered. He tried a third time, but before he could get around, Buck Baker, running more than a full mile *behind* him, crossed the start-finish line, and was declared the winner to raucous cheers—and much to the track officials' satisfaction, according to Scott. The sport's guardians, it seemed, just weren't ready for the spectacle of a black man celebrating in Victory Lane. It was highway robbery, plain and simple.

"Everybody in the place knew I had won that race," a resentful Scott recalled years later. "But the promoters and NASCAR officials didn't want me out there kissing any beauty queens or accepting any awards."

Officials later informed Scott that the blunder was the result of an unfortunate scoring error and awarded him his only Grand National victory hours after the last fans had left. A month later, in Savannah, in a feeble attempt to make amends, NASCAR gave Scott his "trophy"—little more than a varnished wooden post bearing a crudely carved inscription. Baker kept the gleaming original.

But the slight didn't stop Scott from doing what he did best. The 1964 season would turn out to be the winningest of his career—he would cop eight top five showings and twenty-five top tens while running 56 races, and would finish twelfth in overall points.

Scott would continue racing until 1973, when a bad wreck at Talladega left him nearly crippled and in chronic pain.

"He probably did more with less than any driver I've ever seen," said racer Ned Jarrett. "But he just never really got the [financial] break he needed to show the talents that he had....He could have knocked our pants off."

Scott died in 1990 from spinal cancer at the age of sixty-nine. In 1999 he was inducted into the International Motorsports Hall of Fame. He remains the only African American to ever win a race at NASCAR's highest level.

Wendell Scott with Bill France, 1965.

Richard Brickhouse's Day in the Talladega Sun

• • • • • • • • • • •

The sad story of Richard Brickhouse began and ended on a single fall day in 1969. Momentarily raised up as a champion, he'd be dropped like a hot potato, the unfortunate victim of a political battle between forces much greater than himself.

When he came to NASCAR in late 1968 Brickhouse was green, straight off the farm, a dirt racer who'd never touched a paved track. But the talented twenty-seven-year-old managed to turn a few heads with top ten performances at Darlington and Rockingham, running a cast-off 1967 Plymouth purchased from Richard Petty.

Keeping that car going at the Winston Cup level,

however, proved difficult. Without sponsorship, Brickhouse found himself pouring his soybean savings into a quickly sinking ship. And then came Talladega.

The brand-new 2.66-mile Alabama track—the latest jewel in NASCAR boss Big Bill France's crown—was to host the first ever Talladega 500 on September 14, 1969. But there were problems. The track was unbelievably fast, and at 200 mph–plus, the asphalt quickly turned drivers' tires to spaghetti during qualifying.

That was all most racers needed to see. Petty's recently organized Professional Drivers Association (PDA) boycotted the race, and its members, including more than thirty top competitors, packed up their equipment and went home. France was fuming. With less than twenty-four hours before start time, he hit the phones, wheedling, cajoling, and threatening NASCAR's remaining drivers into their cars.

Brickhouse, himself a member of the PDA, had a tough decision. Chrysler had offered him a ride in a factory Dodge vacated by a striking racer—an invitation Brickhouse saw as a stepping-stone to sponsorship.

"I got involved in racing solely for that chance," he would say later. "It was a once-in-a-lifetime opportunity for me."

He broke the boycott.

On Sunday afternoon, Brickhouse, sitting ninth in a motley, thrown-together field of Grand National drivers, minor-league competitors, and rank amateurs, fired up his purple number 99 factory Dodge and hit the frontstretch. To preserve tires, speeds were kept to about 175 mph. But with eleven laps left Brickhouse couldn't restrain himself. He put the hammer down and blasted through the field, taking the checkered by a full seven seconds.

Brickhouse was elated, Chrysler was happy, and Big Bill was positively ecstatic. France joined the beaming Brickhouse in the winner's circle, where he placed a wreath of roses around the newcomer's neck and declared bromidically, "Winners never quit, and quitters never win!"

Brickhouse shines at Talladega.

"I thought I was doing the right thing," Brickhouse said later. "But running that race hurt my career."

In fact, it effectively ended it. When the PDA's top drivers returned to the fold weeks later, Chrysler welcomed them with open arms, and Brickhouse was left out in the cold. The victory that should have been a springboard to a top-notch ride instead became a death knell.

Having forever earned the enmity of NASCAR's best-known drivers, and lacking the cash and connections to stay competitive, Brickhouse would run only thirteen more times before retiring in 1982. He never won again.

Ron Bouchard: A New England Yankee in a Southerners' Sport

• • • • • • • • •

Ron Bouchard liked to think of himself as an anomaly, a New England Yankee in a Southerners' sport, but he had all the bona fides of any 'baccy-chomping, pedal-mashing good ol' boy from the Piedmont plateau.

The son of a long-haul trucker, Bouchard grew up in the dingy Massachussetts mill town of Fitchburg, known more for cultivating football talent than road warriors. But he developed an early passion for speed, fed by his father, who sponsored a team on the local modified circuit.

The story runs that with the elder Bouchard on the road and his ace driver laid low by the flu, fourteen-year-old Ron jumped behind the wheel and piloted the car to victory. From that point on he did little else, winning minor-league stock and modified championships throughout the 1970s.

Bouchard joined the Cup Series ranks in 1981, and over his first ten races quickly established a boom-or-bust pattern—five times the hard-charger either wrecked or trashed engines, the other five he finished in the top ten.

So it was anyone's guess where he'd wind up in the

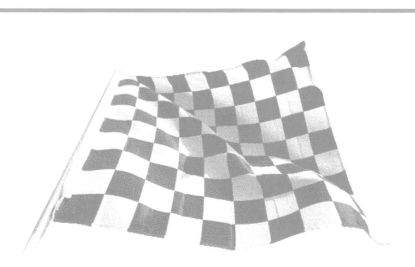

August 2 running of the Talladega 500 at Alabama's notoriously unpredictable superspeedway. Since opening, Talladega had had thirteen winners in thirteen years. Nine of them would be competing against the thirty-two-year-old Bouchard—including heavy hitters Bobby Allison, Darrell Waltrip, Richard Petty, and Neil Bonnett.

Allison managed to put the race in a throttlehold for most of the afternoon, dominating 105 of the 168 laps before engine trouble dampened his fire with just six laps to go. Waltrip then charged to the lead, followed closely by Terry Labonte. Ron Bouchard was in third.

Coming into the race's final turn, Labonte went high to the outside of Waltrip, pulling even. The New England freshman dove low. With 75,000 fans rising for the checkered, they came tearing down the frontstretch neck and neck, three-wide. Bouchard managed to give it just enough, and his number 47 Buick nosed out Waltrip by a foot, Labonte by two. It was one of the closest finishes in NASCAR history.

"They told me it would be impossible to win here," Bouchard said. "But I used positive thinking to keep myself up to believe I could win. It's the happiest day of my life."

Perhaps the gift of positive thinking had a short shelf life. Or maybe the racing gods were just feeling magnanimous that day. Whatever the case, Ron Bouchard would never win again. He would, however, finish in the top ten three more times that season (and 48 more over the next 149 races) and collect 1981 Rookie of the Year honors. His victory made him only the third man since 1957 to win a race as a rookie.

Three months into the 1987 season, Bouchard hung it up, taking his career $1.3 million in earnings back to his native Fitchburg, where he opened a chain of car dealerships. In 1998 he was inducted into the New England Auto Racers Hall of Fame.

Ron Bouchard (47) beats out Waltrip and Allison by a nose.

Mark Donohue: Captain Nice

• • • • • • • • • •

Well into the 1970s NASCAR drivers were still a blue-collar, bluegrass bunch—tough customers from the mills and farms and factory towns of the rugged Southeast, self-taught and self-reliant. That is to say, most of them hadn't graduated from an Ivy League university with a degree in mechanical engineering.

Mark Donohue wasn't most racers.

They might have ribbed Donohue for his crew cut and egghead credentials—he was even tagged with the syrupy sobriquet "Captain Nice" for his mild manner—but when it came time to put the pedal down the Philadelphia-area native and Brown University alum was as hardnosed as anybody in the pomade-and-chaw crowd.

"There was a lot of tiger in Mark," said car designer Carroll Smith. "You know the old story

Mark Donohue celebrates in victory lane after winning the 1973 Winston Western 500 at Riverside Raceway.

about engineers don't make good race drivers because they don't want to hurt the machinery? Bullshit."

By the time Donohue threw his hat into the Cup Series ring in the early '70s, he was already a racing legend, having been named Indy 500 Rookie of the Year (1969) and having won the Indianapolis 500 (1972), the U.S. Road Racing Championship twice ('67 and '68), and the Trans-Am title three times ('68, '69, and '70).

His versatility—he ran road courses and ovals in Camaros, Porsches, Ferraris, Javelins, and McLarens—and his engineering brilliance ("the unfair advantage," one reporter called it) had made him one of the most feared competitors in motor sports. The innovative Donohue could take apart a high-performance machine and rebuild it with his eyes closed, tweaking it just enough to give him the winning edge.

For Captain Nice, NASCAR was just one more mountain demanding to be scaled.

It didn't take long to reach the top. In just his fifth race, at Riverside's 2.6-mile road course, he jumped out to an early lead on past course champions Bobby Allison, Richard Petty, and Ray Elder. Midway through the 191-lap race, Donohue's red, white, and blue number 16 American Motors Matador began to pull away for good.

On January 21, 1973, after nearly five grueling hours of racing—twenty-four of the forty cars died early deaths—Donohue crossed the finish line to take the Winston Western 500, more than a full lap ahead of runner-up Allison and two ahead of third-place Elder. It was a dominating performance, one that signaled the arrival of a potent new force in NASCAR.

But Donohue decided one was enough. After winning the Can-Am title later that year and running just one more Cup contest at Atlanta, he retired from racing. "I'm almost thirty-six and feel that I'm at the absolute top of my abilities," he said. "Now is the time to stop."

Owner Roger Penske would coax him out of retirement a year later to take a run at Formula One racing, but it wasn't to be. While turning practice laps for the Austrian Grand Prix in August 1975, Donohue lost control of his car, flew off the track, and smashed into a utility pole. He never regained consciousness and died at the age of thirty-eight.

Shorty Rollins: NASCAR's First Ever Rookie of the Year

●　●　●　●　●　●　●　●　●

Lloyd "Shorty" Rollins's NASCAR career was as brief as his nickname might indicate, but the Texas speedballer didn't need a whole lot of time to make a big splash in the racing world.

As a grocer in Corpus Christi in the late 1950s, Rollins had taken up racing for kicks, running Acapulco-to-El Paso rallies with his brother and mechanic, Dub, before turning his lead foot loose on the quarter-mile clays.

By 1957 he had run circles around the competition four years straight in the Southwest Late Model Series and decided that driving fast and turning left beat the heck out of hawking cucumbers for a living. In early 1958 he packed up the family and headed east for Fayetteville, North Carolina, to try to turn a few bucks on the wild and woolly NASCAR circuit.

With dismal showings in his first three starts, Rollins wondered if maybe he should have stuck to minding the store. But top ten finishes in the next ten races convinced him, along with the rest of the NASCAR field, that he belonged with the big boys.

On July 16, 1958, he would plunk down his calling card at tiny State Line Speedway in Busti, New York, beating out twenty-two others, including defending points champion Lee Petty, for his first Grand National victory.

Rollins would finish the season fourth in points

(close behind future Hall of Famers Petty and Buck Baker), with twelve top five finishes and twenty-two top tens, after running just twenty-nine of the year's fifty-one races. His muscular driving earned him more than $13,000, as well as NASCAR's first ever Rookie of the Year award.

Rollins's 1958 win at Busti would be his last, at least in a points race. But he's perhaps better known for his February 10, 1959, non-points victory in a 100-mile convertible qualifier for the inaugural Daytona 500. After scrambling to drop a borrowed engine into his Ford, Shorty barely made it to the start line before the green flag dropped.

Rollins, Glen Wood, Marvin Panch, and twenty-one-year-old rookie Richard Petty would pass the lead around five times over the last ten laps before Shorty bogarted it, edging out Wood and Petty by less than a car length. In doing so, he secured a place in the record books as the first driver to win at the now legendary track.

Two days later, the twenty-nine-year-old rising star fried his motor halfway through the 500. Beset by mechanical problems, he would run only nine more races that year, and just four more the next, never regaining the magic of his debut season.

In September 1960, Rollins bid goodbye to

Rollins, Glen Wood, Marvin Panch, and the rookie Richard Petty would pass the lead around five times over the last 10 laps before Shorty bogarted it, edging out Wood and Petty by less than a car-length. In doing so, he secured a place in the record books as the first driver to win at the now legendary track.

NASCAR for good, retiring with his family to Pensacola, Florida, where he ran a successful fence business until his death in 1998.

"My wife and I decided it wasn't the kind of life we wanted," Rollins said. "It was great for the single guys out there, but not for me."

Phil Parsons: Victim of the Talladega Curse

• • • • • • • • • •

Superstitions run deep in NASCAR. Over the years drivers have engaged in endless hand-wringing over the jinx potential of green cars, peanuts, women in the pits, and a host of other vexing agents of voodoo. By the late 1980s Talladega Superspeedway had joined that list, with a hexology all its own.

Not only was the Alabama track notorious for its harrowing multicar pileups and deadly freak accidents off the oval, it also harbored a "kiss of death" for first-time winners. By 1987 all four drivers who had logged their first Cup victory at Talladega since 1969

had left the sport without winning again. Bobby Hillin Jr., who visited Victory Lane in 1986, would eventually suffer the same fate.

Driver Phil Parsons was no stranger to the track's treacherousness. In 1983, his first year in Cup competition, he'd nearly given up the ghost when his Pontiac flipped and burst into flames, precipitating a massive eleven-car wreck. He escaped with a cracked shoulder blade. But five years later to the day he would come face-to-face with the curse.

The Detroit native and younger brother of racer

Benny Parsons was enjoying the best season of his career in 1988. He'd had one top five and four top ten showings in the first eight races and would eventually finish ninth in the points. What he didn't have was a win. Not in 1988, not ever. But he loved racing at Talladega, and with a powerful Leo Jackson Oldsmobile under him, he figured he had his best shot yet in May's Winston 500.

His assumptions proved correct. Parsons would lead 37 laps early before dropping back to conserve energy for a late-race charge. Running second behind Geoff Bodine with 50 laps to go, he radioed his crew, asking cockily, "Should I blow his doors off now or should I wait?" He'd grant Bodine 15 further laps of daylight before leaving him in a cloud of dust, and would then hold off a final tail-whacking challenge from a game Bobby Allison (who collapsed in exhaustion after the race) to capture his first win by 0.21 seconds.

"I've always loved this racetrack," he told reporters afterwards. "I loved it before the accident in 1983 and I loved it before we won today. This is my favorite racetrack and always has been."

Had Parsons known what black fate Talladega had in store for him, he might have reconsidered his unbridled declarations of love. For, like the five unfortunate souls before him, Faithful Phil would find himself eternally iced out of the winner's circle, condemned to wallow in NASCAR's backfields for the remainder of his ninety-two races, until his retirement in 1997.

Parsons would, however, continue to run in NASCAR's

Busch Series, winning not once but *twice* in sixteen years of competition. He would eventually follow his more famous brother, Benny, into broadcasting, working as a television race analyst for NASCAR's Craftsman Truck Series.

Talladega has not claimed another first-timer. Yet.

Phil Parsons holds the winners trophy after taking the checkered flag in the Winston 500 at Talladega.

Lake Speed: A Banner Day at Darlington

• • • • • • • • • •

NASCAR driver Lake Speed notched a few quirky "firsts" during his racing career. He was the first American to win a World Karting Championship, he was the first to pilot the campy Hormel-bankrolled Ford known as the SPAM-o-nator, and he was one of the first born-again Christian racers to openly engage in trackside proselytizing.

And at Darlington Raceway on March 27, 1988, after nearly nine years of failed attempts, he collected his very first Cup Series win—a fact interesting only in that it would also be his last.

Which isn't to say that this son of Jackson, Mississippi, didn't run close to the pack's alpha dogs. After all, when your last name is your profession, you'd better be good at what you do. Over a career spanning nineteen years and 402 races, Speed managed to log seventy-five top ten finishes—including a second-place nail-biter at the 1985 Daytona 500, where he lost by just 0.94 seconds—and earn more than $4.5 million.

But he was also one of the sport's perpetual dark horses, a friendly aw-shucks gentleman who hit more than a few bad patches along the road and never complained.

After being canned by the RahMoc race team in early 1986, the thirty-eight-year-old father of four marshaled all his assets and started his own operation. It was tough going. Speed sat out the remainder of '86 and raced only a limited schedule in '87. But by '88 he'd secured sponsorship and was back in the game.

"It's been a long, tough struggle. It's never been easy," he said. "Sometimes I began to wonder if I was ever going to make it."

But there he was, lined up at Darlington for the fifth race of the season, just three weeks after posting the second red-ribbon finish of his career, at Rockingham. Things were looking up.

Speed, starting eighth, managed to avoid two nasty multicar wrecks in the TranSouth 500's early going and began methodically working his way to the front.

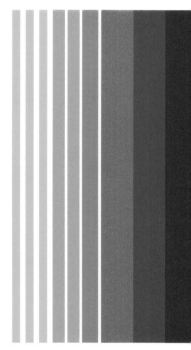

By Lap 319 of 367, Speed was running second behind Sterling Marlin, who went in for tires. But a bungled pit held Marlin back, giving Speed plenty of breathing room with 49 laps to go. Alan Kulwicki took over second, but windshield visibility problems kept him from mounting a serious challenge.

He'd get there three times before falling back, but stayed cozy with the leaders as the point changed hands an additional fourteen times.

By Lap 319 of 367, Speed was running second behind Sterling Marlin, who went in for tires. But a bungled pit held Marlin back, giving Speed plenty of breathing room with 49 laps to go. Alan Kulwicki took over second, but windshield visibility problems kept him from mounting a serious challenge. By the time Speed reached the finish, he'd put a full 19 seconds between himself and Kulwicki, and Davey Allison, Bill Elliott, and Marlin came in 3-4-5.

"To win that first race is a tremendous relief," Speed said afterwards. "I always knew I had the ability to do it."

On Monday, Speed's garage was bombarded with congratulatory calls from well-wishers. "It was good and great to get that first win, but it isn't anything real different," he'd say after all the adulation. "My life's not going to change."

Buddy Shuman: A Legend in His Own Time

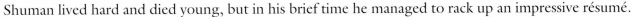

Buddy Shuman was a true NASCAR character, a good-time Charlie whose diminutive stature was eclipsed by a larger-than-life personality and whose legend far outlasted his short career.

Shuman lived hard and died young, but in his brief time he managed to rack up an impressive résumé. He was an ace mechanic, a successful driver, a car owner, a NASCAR inspection official, and an automotive design liaison to the Ford Motor Company, in addition to being a notorious carouser with a firm devotion to Canadian whiskey.

Like many in NASCAR's pioneer class, Shuman made his early bread as a bootlegger, albeit one whose failure to outrun the law earned him a bullet through the neck and a free pass to a North Carolina chain gang.

Upon his release, Shuman joined the ranks of Bruton Smith's fledgling National Stock Car Racing Association, under whose auspices he won dozens of modified races and nabbed the 1948 stock car championship. As his reputation grew, he was courted by Big Bill France, whose NASCAR organization, formed in 1947, was battling Smith's for control of the Southeastern tracks.

A true NASCAR character, Shuman lived every day to the fullest.

When Smith's operation folded in 1951, Shuman brought his considerable talent to NASCAR and in his debut Grand National season scored a perfect seven top ten finishes in seven races. He also quickly gained renown as an affable dipsomaniac and jaw-wagger, always good for a droll quote.

When asked by a reporter how he handled the difficult track at Darlington, Shuman unabashedly replied, "I take the car through the straightaways, and Lord Calvert [whiskey] takes her through the turns."

Whether or not Lord Calvert was copiloting Shuman's ride during NASCAR's first venture onto Canadian turf, in 1952, will remain a mystery, but the thirty-seven-year-old speedster ran like canned heat over the half-mile Stamford Park horse track at Niagara Falls. Shuman led the final 64 swings of the 200-lapper to take the victory in his '52 Hudson Hornet by two full laps over future Hall of Famer Herb Thomas. Eleven of the race's seventeen starters watched the final action of the wreckful contest from the sidelines.

Shuman collected a grand for the win and $4,210 for his fifteen races and seven top ten finishes that year. But his responsibilities as a mechanic and a NASCAR inspector kept him from running much, and over the next three years he'd compete only seven times. Shuman's Niagara victory would remain the only win in his twenty-seven-race NASCAR career.

By 1955 the forty-year-old retired racer would be working with Ford to develop a competitive answer to Chevy's dominance on the Grand National circuit when he was burned to death in a Hickory, North Carolina, hotel room. It was an exit some attributed to a lethal combination of nightcaps and bedtime smokes.

In 1957 NASCAR introduced the annual Buddy Shuman Memorial Award to honor individuals whose efforts on and off the track have contributed to the advancement of NASCAR competition.

Jim Hurtubise: Racing's Lazarus
● ● ● ● ● ● ● ● ●

In this era of drive-thru nose jobs and on-demand tummy tucks, body alteration has become as commonplace as dew in Dixie. But racer Jim "Hercules" Hurtubise is probably the only man to ever have his hands molded to fit a steering wheel.

"People said I was nuts having my hands that way," Hurtubise once said, "but auto racing was the way I earned my living, the only thing I could do and the only thing I wanted to do."

Hurtubise's hands and face had been horribly disfigured in a fiery Indy-car crash in 1964, along with half his body, and the driver spent an excruciating year in the hospital, undergoing dozens of painful skin grafts and physical therapy to restore what was left of his skin and muscle tissue. Though told at the outset he would never race again, the thirty-one-year-old demanded that doctors surgically sculpt his mangled hands to allow him to grip a wheel.

Hurtubise had never been one to let go of a dream. Throughout the late 1950s, the New Yorker had traveled state to state, looking for sprint car competition and living out of the trunk of his Pontiac. When he finally got the call from Indy in 1960, the young wolf took a big bite out of the Brickyard, winning Rookie of the Year honors for his qualifying performance in the 500 and becoming a fast crowd favorite for his take-no-prisoners, pit-bull attitude on the track.

Despite horrific injury, Hurtubise rides again.

"The people just loved him," said fellow racer Parnelli Jones. "They knew he never sandbagged. He drove as hard as he could, even if the car was a dog."

Those fans stood gape-jawed when, just weeks out of recovery, Hurtubise rejoined the open-wheel circuit. But while he ran strong on occasion, he didn't seem to have the old knack. Having spun a few Grand National races in the years preceding his crash, Hurtubise decided to shift his attention to NASCAR.

He started the 1966 season with a sixth-place finish at Riverside and followed with a fourth at the Daytona 500. By then his folk status was growing and everyone

As he made his way to Victory Lane, Hurtubise received an extended standing ovation from the crowd of 71,000.

"I never saw anything like that day, because most of the fans hollering had tears running down their cheeks," Petty recalled. "Only race I ever ran when I was almost glad I didn't win."

Hurtubise would run Indy and stock cars (including twenty-five NASCAR Cup races) until 1978 but would never win again. He died of a heart attack in 1989.

Frankie Schneider: The Old Master at Old Dominion

● ● ● ● ● ● ● ● ●

Few individuals outside of politics and kung-fu movies can carry a nickname like "The Old Master" with a straight face. Frankie Schneider is one of them.

During his thirty-year career, Schneider won more car races than anyone who ever strapped on a seatbelt. The exact figures are hazy, but it's estimated that from 1947 to 1977, the former New Jersey farmer copped nearly 750 checkered flags, including a mind-boggling 100 in 1958 alone. His secret?

"I'd run anything there was."

Whether midgets, sprints, late models, stockers, or his particular specialty, modifieds, it made no difference. He'd run on dirt, clay, asphalt, grass, on half-miles, quarter-miles, and bullrings. If there was a race on, Schneider was there, seven days a week and twice on Sundays.

But there was more to his success than sheer quantity. Schneider, quite simply, was an exceedingly smart driver. Eschewing the hard-charging, blood-and-sheet-metal style so prevalent on the early dirt tracks, Schneider opted for safety and stamina, carefully side-stepping his way through minefields and preserving his ride for late-race runs, when he'd sail smoothly

wanted to see this racing Lazarus pull one out.

They got their wish three weeks later on March 27, at the Atlanta 500. In a hard-fought 334-lap battle that saw only seventeen of forty-four cars finish, Hurtubise jousted for the lead with top guns Richard Petty, David Pearson, Curtis Turner, and Ned Jarrett before rocketing over the last 120 laps to win, leaving runner-up Fred Lorenzen nearly two miles behind.

past the bashed and wheezing wrecks of his competitors.

"I think I was just a better driver, and a good mechanic," he once explained of his longevity.

The conservative approach served him well, helping him capture NASCAR's Modified championship in 1952, a year in which he won nearly ninety races, and Eastern States titles in 1962, '63, and '67.

While known primarily as a modified driver, Schneider did make forays into NASCAR's Grand National ranks. He ran nineteen races between 1949 and 1957, lodging six top five finishes and ten top tens, including one close run at Raleigh in 1957 that was hampered by race officials.

"I remember my gasman got thrown out of the pits because he wasn't sixteen years old yet," Schneider recalled. "So when I came in for stops, I got out of the car and refueled it myself. I think I still finished second."

He'd have no such problems at Old Dominion Speedway on April 25, 1958. After letting his colleagues overheat and blow transmissions while blistering around the 0.38-mile track for 44 laps, Schneider moved into position and grabbed the point. Despite the best efforts of Lee Petty, Rex White, and Junior Johnson, that's exactly where his '57 Chevy would remain. One hundred and six laps and a half-hour later, Schneider had his first, and only, Grand National victory.

1958 would be Schneider's best year in a stock car. In addition to his Old Dominion win, he would finish top five four times in just seven races. But his $1,970 overall take wouldn't be enough to keep him going past May.

"I was a low-buck guy my entire career," the independent, unsponsored Schneider explained. "I quit Grand Nationals because it was too expensive."

Modifieds presented a more lucrative return on his investment, and that's where the Old Master went, finishing out his typically busy year with an astounding 100 wins.

NASCAR'S DYNASTIES

Before long Ned Jarrett was racing regularly
under an assumed name—until his father Homer found out.
Resigned to his son's newfound ambition, he made only
one request: If you're going to win, use the family name.

The France Family: NASCAR's First Family

• • • • • • • • • •

In August 1961 a group of well-known racers, backed by Jimmy Hoffa's Teamsters, presented NASCAR boss Bill France with a list of demands. They wanted a union. They wanted better purses, a pension plan, and a scholarship fund for deceased drivers' children. They wanted a hand in running things.

Fat chance. France threatened to plow up his prized Daytona Speedway and plant corn in the infield before he would allow anyone to meddle with his personal fiefdom. He immediately expelled the ringleaders from NASCAR for life. Then he really laid down the law. "No known Teamster can compete in a NASCAR race," he stated flatly. "And I'll enforce that with a pistol."

There was no sense challenging Big Bill. Whether it was his size—he stood six foot five and weighed about 250 pounds—his self-professed skill with a firearm, or his wily political machinations, France managed to impose his will on drivers, auto manufacturers, track owners, and race promoters for more than twenty-five years while transforming a rowdy, backwoods bootleggers' craze into the most popular racing series in the country.

"It's true France was tough," said Richard Petty, whose own drivers' union was busted by Big Bill in the late 1960s. "I didn't agree with a lot of the things he did. And what NASCAR did usually reflected what the old man wanted. But what he did for stock car racing and auto racing in general cannot be denied."

In the mid-1940s the sport was in its infancy, and it was a mess. At scores of small tracks throughout the Southeast, the same scenes were repeated: crooked race promoters flew the coop with prize money; rankled drivers bludgeoned each other with tire irons; drunken

Bill France Jr. watches during the NASCAR Nextel Cup Series Chevy American Revolution 400 on Mary 15, 2004 at Richmond International Raceway in Richmond, Virginia.

(*Overleaf*): **Dale Jarrett wins the UAW Ford 500 NASCAR race at the Talladega Super Speedway in Talladega, Alabama.**

(*Left*): **Bill France with Lee Petty.**

fans fired pistols and heaved bottles, chicken bones, and sometimes each other, onto the track. Cheating was rampant. Dozens of sanctioning bodies made competing claims to "national" preeminence, a good many of them nothing more than letterhead on cheap stationery.

Into the chaos galloped France, part P. T. Barnum, part John Wayne, part Machiavellian prince. France knew the score; he'd been promoting contests on the Daytona sands since 1938 and competing himself since

NASCAR Chairman and CEO Brian France stands in front of NASCAR's home office in Daytona Beach, Florida. Brian was handed the reins of the business after his father, Bill France Jr., stepped down in 2003.

his youth in Washington, D.C. If "redneck racin' " was ever going to succeed on a national stage, Big Bill figured, he'd have to do it.

And so in late 1947, at the Streamline Hotel in Daytona Beach, the thirty-eight-year-old gas station owner and mechanic announced the formation of NASCAR (National Association for Stock Car Auto Racing), with himself as majority owner and sole governing sultan. The new sheriff quickly implemented a set of uniform rules for competition, developed a clear-cut points system to determine an annual champion, and personally guaranteed the purses. With a circuit of tracks in the fold, NASCAR ran its first all-stock race in June 1949. Big Bill never looked back.

Over the next two decades France would grow the sport like hothouse flowers, expanding into new states, building state-of-the-art tracks (including his hallowed temple at Daytona), courting the deep pockets of Detroit's auto manufacturers, and making himself and a number of lead-footed good ol' boys stinking rich.

France's success went a long way toward muzzling his critics, but his outsize personality and dictatorial approach—racers liked to joke that his board meetings were held in a phone booth—didn't always sit right with Detroit, or the hard-boiled collection of whiskey runners, dirt farmers, and Dixie daredevils who made up a large chunk of racing's early talent pool. But the NASCAR pie belonged to Bill, and if you wanted a piece, you had to quit sniveling and play by his rules.

After all, if you pushed him, he pushed back harder—and he was never above adding a dramatic flourish to drive home the message. In 1969, when Richard Petty's budding drivers' association threatened to boycott the inaugural race at France's newly built Talladega Speedway over track safety issues, Big Bill scoffed and took a few blistering swings around the oval before opining, "If a sixty-year-old man can drive 176 mph around the track, surely our top drivers can do it safely at twenty miles over that."

By the time France handed control of the empire to his son Bill Jr. in 1972, NASCAR had burst out of its small-time Southern shackles to become a multimillion-dollar enterprise and a growing national phenomenon.

Under the three generations of the France family, NASCAR has exploded with record attendance.

With the help of his son Brian and daughter Lesa, Bill Jr. would turn it into a bona fide American institution.

Under Bill Jr.'s three-decade tenure, the sport exploded, fueled by millions in corporate sponsorship, mega-dollar television contracts, and attendance that topped four million annually by 2000. The stars of the 1970s, '80s, and '90s—drivers like Richard Petty, Dale Earnhardt, and Jeff Gordon—became household names, and race purses and driver contracts began to resemble the gross national product of small countries.

And while Bill Jr. may not have had the kiss-my-ring mien of his father, he had the savvy and smarts to ensure that all of racing's competing interests generally walked away happy, or at least equally ticked off.

"Bill [had] a tremendous ability to make all the people in this sport see the big picture...that if we do things a certain way, everybody wins," Mike Helton, NASCAR's president, said of his boss.

Today, with Big Bill's grandson Brian France at the helm, the $3-billion-a-year company has expanded into every region of the country—the premier Cup Series runs on twenty-three tracks in nineteen different states—and continues to court an ever-growing fan base, which NASCAR pegs at more than 75 million. NASCAR is second only to the NFL in popularity, and its ubiquitous corporate logo can be found on everything from T-shirts to supermarket broccoli.

With the third generation of Frances steering the family ship, Bill Jr. takes comfort in knowing that whatever changes the years ahead may bring, NASCAR will persevere.

Unashamedly aware of his legacy, Big Bill once prophetically proclaimed, "This thing will be growing and full of life long after I'm gone."

The Pettys: NASCAR's Royal Family

• • • • • • • • • •

It's a little-told tale, but the Petty dynasty started with a resounding thud. In 1949, Lee Petty entered NASCAR's first ever stock event, a 150-mile dirt-track race in Charlotte. His eyes set on the $5,000 purse, Lee ran hard—so hard he flipped his borrowed 1946 Buick Roadmaster four times, sending it to the boneyard.

"He tore it all to pieces," recalled Richard Petty, who'd made the 100-mile trip from their home in Randleman, North Carolina, with

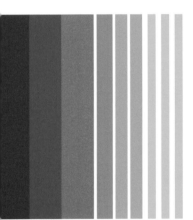

In 1949, Lee Petty entered NASCAR's first-ever stock event, a 150-mile dirt-track race in Charlotte. His eyes set on the $5,000 purse, Lee ran hard— so hard he flipped his borrowed 1946 Buick Roadmaster four times, sending it to the boneyard.

his father. "Turned out we didn't have a way home." So while Lee stayed behind to mop up the mess, twelve-year-old Richard was obliged to thumb his way back to the farm and explain to Mama Petty how Pops had turned the neighbors' family sedan into a toaster.

So much for auspicious beginnings, but it hardly mattered. When all was said and done, that opening-day disaster would become a quaint footnote in NASCAR's greatest family epic, a saga encompassing four generations of drivers, 2,385 races, 263 wins, 8 Daytona 500 victories, 10 championships, and 1,230 top ten finishes.

By the time Lee retired from racing in 1964—the same year

Kyle Petty, center, holds the trophy with help from his grandfather Lee Petty, left, and father, Richard, second from right as the Petty family celebrates in victory lane in Daytona, Florida, after Kyles' first racing win in this 1979 photo provided by the Richard Petty Museum.

Richard logged his first championship—he'd won more races (54) and captured more points titles (3) than any other driver. But those marks would soon be wiped from the books, as Richard, playing Hammerin' Hank to Lee's Babe Ruth, raised the bar and forever established himself as "the King" of stock car racing.

From the mid-1960s to the early 1980s, Richard marauded over the competition—despite gritty opposition from stars like David Pearson, Cale Yarborough, and Bobby Allison—and accomplished feats that still leave race fans slack-jawed, setting all-time records for victories (200), Cup titles (7), single-season wins (27), consecutive wins (10), Daytona 500s (7), and poles (126).

As NASCAR grew, so did the King's legend, and there was hardly a red-blooded American who didn't recognize the mustachioed dude with the oversized shades, feathered Stetson, and red-and-white number 43 car as NASCAR's high priest of speed and goodwill ambassador.

When Richard's son Kyle took up the family mantle in 1979, for the simple reason, Kyle said, that he "was too lazy to work and too chicken to steal," it was clear there would be no regicide. Although he garnered a respectable eight wins and fifty-one top five finishes over twenty-six years—and continues to compete in the Cup Series—he liked to joke that "the genes for [driving] skill must have skipped a generation," citing his own son Adam as the true heir to the Petty throne.

Tragically, Adam Petty never got a chance to prove his mettle. After running only one Cup race, in 2000, the nineteen-year-old was killed in a practice-run crash at New Hampshire.

Richard and Kyle continue to operate the Petty Enterprises race team, hoping that someday Kyle's younger son, Austin, might step up to carry the flame for a fourth generation. "This is what the Pettys have always done, as a family," said Kyle. "You just keep plugging along."

The Allisons: NASCAR's "Alabama Gang"

• • • • • • • • •

Davey Allison had lost the biggest race of his young career and it was the happiest day of his life. The twenty-seven-year-old phenom was pleased as peaches finishing second in the 1988 Daytona 500 because the old man who'd smoked him on the final lap happened to be his hero—Davey's father Bobby.

Bobby Allison could be forgiven for the burn. That's just the way he was, and everybody knew it: stubborn, hot-blooded, and fervently dedicated to winning. One didn't rack up eighty-four victories—third on NASCAR's all-time list—by letting a little thing like genes muck up a hard charge to the checkered flag. Even Bobby's sibling and fellow driver Donnie, no pushover himself, had been victimized more than once by his brother's "love taps."

Long before they'd moved from Miami to Alabama and exploded onto the Grand National scene in the mid-1960s, the cantankerous Allison brothers had

earned a reputation as gritty small-track competitors who rumbled as well as they raced. And boy, could they race. Donnie, who won NASCAR Rookie of the Year honors in 1967, repeated the feat at the Indianapolis 500 just three years later.

But it was Bobby, 1983's NASCAR Cup champion, who put the Allison stamp on NASCAR. His 336 top five finishes over a twenty-five-year career were second only to his archrivals, Richard Petty and David Pearson. And unlike those easygoing aces, Bobby became as famous for his nasty temper as for his talent on the track.

"Bobby was combative," said Humpy Wheeler, president of Lowe's Speedway. "He was a tremendous, tremendous competitor. There was nothing hidden about it."

It certainly wasn't hidden during Bobby and Donnie's bloody televised brawl with Cale Yarborough on the Daytona infield in 1979. After Cale and Donnie

Bobby Allison gives advice to his brother Donnie.

wrecked while bumping hard for the lead in the 500, brotherly Bobby pulled on the scene to settle the beef. "I got out," he recalled poetically, "and old Cale went to beating on my fist with his nose."

Davey Allison hadn't inherited Bobby's tough-guy bravado, but no doubt he had his daddy's racing blood. After winning Rookie of the Year in 1987, he went on to post nineteen victories over the next six seasons. The thirty-three-year-old was being touted as NASCAR's next superstar when a helicopter crash ended his life in 1993.

For Bobby, still semi-incapacitated by the career-

1988 Daytona 500 winner Bobby Allison pours beer on son Davey during celebrations.

ending 1988 wreck that left him with crushed legs, a shattered skull, and permanent memory loss, Davey's death only compounded his overwhelming grief—he'd lost his younger son Clifford just eleven months earlier in a Busch Series crash.

But if tragedy seemed to follow the Allison's "Alabama Gang"—a mere seven months after Davey, fellow member Neil Bonnett would also die in a crash—their triumphs on the track over more than three decades elevated them to racing immortality. Together, the Allison family ran 862 races (notching an astonishing 653 top ten finishes) and graced Victory Lane 144 times, making them, behind the Pettys, the winningest clan in NASCAR history.

The Woods: NASCAR's Oldest Team

• • • • • • • • •

To say that Glen and Leonard Wood knew how to run a race team is a little like saying Picasso knew how to paint—it doesn't do justice to the scope of their talent. Truth is, during the first thirty-odd years of NASCAR's existence, these two brothers from the sleepy boondocks of Stuart, Virginia, not only put more top-flight drivers behind the wheel than anyone else, they completely revolutionized the way races were run.

"Leonard and Glen were among the first to attack things scientifically," said driver Dan Gurney, who drove for the Woods in the mid-1960s. "They practiced everything, looking for efficiency and every little advantage. But they downplayed their abilities, like quiet hillbilly types."

It was precisely that fusion of technical wizardry and their humble, homespun approach—they preferred doing business with a handshake—that brought the likes of Curtis Turner, Joe Weatherly, Junior Johnson, Marvin Panch, A. J. Foyt, Cale Yarborough, and David Pearson to their doorstep. Seventeen of NASCAR's 50 Great Drivers had raced for the Woods (including Glen himself, from 1953 to 1964).

But driving talent counts for little if a crew can't deliver, and here the Woods, who pitted every race themselves, decimated the competition. During the early 1960s, the idea of changing four tires and pumping 22 gallons of fuel in 20 seconds seemed absurd. The Woods did it regularly. They developed fuel flow modifications, invented faster lug-nut threading techniques, improved pneumatic air wrenches, and choreographed their movements, anything to get an edge.

"People wasn't taking it very serious about pit stops," recalled Glen. "And we started concentrating on it. We would make a stop and come out a half-lap ahead."

That quickness could often mean the difference in a race, something the Woods discovered early, when their 17-second stops and brilliant fuel management helped Tiny Lund win the 1963 Daytona 500. Lund, leading with ten laps to go, was passed by Fred Lorenzen and Ned Jarrett; both then pitted for fuel. But Lund had enough left to charge on, retaking the lead and sputtering out of gas just seconds after crossing the finish line. And the Woods never *once* changed the tires!

By 1985, when Glen turned over ownership of the team to his sons after thirty-five years in business, the Wood Brothers had earned 269 top five finishes and 92 victories with twelve different drivers (fourth on the all-time list), including four Daytona 500s and a record 80 superspeedway wins.

But the ensuing two decades proved rocky for Wood Brothers Racing, now the oldest continuously operating team in NASCAR. They've visited Victory Lane only five times, and their moderately funded single-car operation has struggled to stay afloat as multicar teams backed by corporate millions have taken over the ranks. But Glen's son, Eddie, has faith they will somehow turn the corner and restore the glory.

"We've had so many ends of the world," he said, "but then it always works out."

Hendrick: The Empire That Rick Built

• • • • • • • • • •

When Rick Hendrick arrived at Daytona International Speedway for his first NASCAR race in 1984, the thirty-six-year-old self-described "redneck car dealer" from Virginia felt like an interloper in the Valley of the Gods. Sure, he'd managed to put together a bare-bones team with the renowned Harry Hyde as crew chief and himself as owner. But he had no major sponsors. He had zero Cup Series experience. And at that moment, he had even less hope.

"I remember looking down pit road...and seeing Richard Petty and [Cale] Yarborough and Junior Johnson and the Wood Brothers and feeling like, 'Man, I don't belong here,' " he recalled.

Today, it's hard to imagine Rick Hendrick belonging anywhere else. Over the past two decades,

the racing dream he hatched with a single car in a small North Carolina garage has grown into one of the richest and most dominant operations in NASCAR history. His Cup teams—now totaling four cars—have amassed 140 overall wins (second on NASCAR's all-time owners list), earned nearly $180 million, and captured five NASCAR Cup championships, including

(*Above*): **Hendrick Motorsports driver Jimmie Johnson (*center*) poses with the winners trophy with co-owners Rick Hendrick and Jeff Gordon in victory lane after winning the NASCAR Winston Clup Series NAPA Auto Parts 500 at the California Speedway in Fontana, California on April 28, 2002.**

an amazing four in a row (1995–98) by Jeff Gordon and Terry Labonte.

Then again, Hendrick has always had a habit of surviving—and thriving—despite the odds. When he spent his last dime to buy a dinky car dealership in 1977, people questioned his sanity; he turned around and built a coast-to-coast empire worth $2 billion a year. When he was told multicar Cup teams were owner suicide, he *expanded* his operation and quickly set a new standard for mutlicar chemistry and competitiveness, all while overcoming both leukemia and a stint of house arrest for mail fraud (he was pardoned in 2000).

But nothing has defined Hendrick's resilience and dedication to racing more than his harrowing 2004 season. What had begun as a yearlong celebration of his twentieth anniversary in NASCAR became a personal and organizational catastrophe when a plane carrying his brother John (the team president), his son Ricky, his two nieces, and his team's general manager and chief engine builder crashed into a foggy hillside in southern Virginia. There were no survivors.

"I love this sport," an emotional Hendrick told the press less than a week after the tragedy. "To honor all of those people on that plane, I am more committed to this sport than I ever have been."

Two days later, Hendrick's four cars rolled up to the starting line at Atlanta Motor Speedway, each bearing pictures of the crash victims. In a fitting tribute, Hendrick driver Jimmie Johnson took the checkered flag in front of 104,000 sympathetic fans.

Johnson and teammate Jeff Gordon would finish the 2004 season second and third, respectively, in the points standings, and by 2005, they would continue to feed off Hendrick's inspiration, finishing fifth and eleventh.

"We were always a family, but I feel like we have a tighter bond with the family," Gordon said. "We all came together in a way that we've stepped up to another level because of [the tragedy]."

"It's incredible how they've been able to survive," said driver Joe Nemechek. "But look at the kind of organization Rick built...that's why it's been able to be strong and continue and be right there at the top of their game."

The Jarretts:
A Championship Family
• • • • • • • • •

"**P**eople who race cars are either bootleggers or fools," Homer Jarrett told his son Ned when the teenager floated the idea of turning a few laps at the local track in the early 1950s.

Well, Ned wasn't a bootlegger. But he had won a half-stake in a race car during a poker game, and despite his parents' notion that a decent boy with a comfortable future in the family's sawmilling operation had no business cavorting with a bunch of hotdogging lowlifes, Ned decided to make a fool of himself.

Before long he was racing regularly under an assumed name and earning quite a reputation in their corner of North Carolina—until Homer found out.

Dale Jarrett, center, poses with his family after winning the NASCAR Winston Cup Series championship Sunday, November 14, 1999, at the Homestead-Miami Speedway in Homestead, Florida. Jarrett finished fifth in the Pennzoil Race to clinch the championship. From left, father, two-time Winston Cup champion Ned, daughter Karsyn, mother Martha, Jarrett, daughter Natalee, son Zachary, wife Kelley and brother Glenn.

Resigned to his son's newfound ambition, he made only one request: if you're going to win, use the family name.

By the time Ned's own son Dale reached his teenage years in the late '70s, the Jarrett name was legendary. In Ned's brief career—he ran only six complete seasons in NASCAR (1960–65), retiring at age thirty-four to become a broadcaster—"Gentleman Ned" won an astonishing fifty races and two Grand National titles, never finishing worse than fifth in the points standings in full-season competition. For Ned, it was all about focus, intensity, and consistency.

Dale had none of that. He'd turned down a university golf scholarship because he didn't like homework. When Ned got him a job as groundskeeper at a racetrack, Dale brought in a herd of goats to assume his lawn-mowing duties. But then Dale got behind the wheel of a race car and something clicked. He would make his full-season Cup debut in 1988.

By 1993's Daytona 500, thirty-six-year-old Dale had won only once. Ned, who was in the booth calling the race for CBS, admitted he had a good feeling about this race, and Dale didn't disappoint. With two laps to go, he made his move on leader Dale Earnhardt, and Ned suddenly found himself cheering his son to victory in front of a national television audience.

"None of the fifty races that I won...gave me the great feeling that I have right now," a beaming Ned said after the race. "To have my son win is the ultimate feeling."

The victory would mark a turning point for Dale. He would win thirty-races over the next twelve seasons (including two more Daytona 500s), finish top five in points seven times, and capture the 1999 Winston Cup championship, making the Jarretts only the second father-son duo to accomplish that feat. Today, Ned is tenth, Dale nineteenth, on NASCAR's all-time win list.

Old Homer would've smiled.

The Flocks: NASCAR's Wild Bunch

● ● ● ● ● ● ● ● ●

In the annals of motor sports there is only one team that ever employed a monkey as a co-driver on the Grand National circuit, only one whose racer outran Johnny Law *in the middle* of a race, and only one with a Cadillac-driving homemaker who whipped NASCAR's biggest names at Daytona. Ladies and gentlemen, meet the incomparable Flying Flocks.

For the first decade of NASCAR's existence, siblings Bob, Fonty, Ethel, and Tim (and occasional simian counterpart Jocko Flocko) provided the burgeoning sport with enough high jinks, political scandal, and good, hard racing to last a lifetime. Between them they ran 381 races, won 63 times, logged 230 top ten finishes, and incurred one lifetime ban. Not bad for a bunch of Alabama bootleggers.

By the late 1940s the Flocks reigned as one of the fastest whiskey-running clans in the South. The frustrated authorities took to ambushing the brothers at local tracks, once barreling into a race in progress,

with sirens blaring, in an attempt to collar Bob, who promptly missed a turn, smashed through a gate, and ran on through downtown Atlanta.

But with the formation of NASCAR in 1947, the Flocks had a chance to go straight. In 1949, the first full year of competition, Bob, Fonty, and Tim gave the family name marquee status by each finishing in the top ten in points. Even their hard-charging sister Ethel chipped in, besting both Fonty and Bob—along with future Hall of Famers Curtis Turner, Herb Thomas, and Buck Baker—with an eleventh-place finish at that year's Daytona race.

While Bob and Ethel rarely raced in the coming years and Fonty (known for his peculiar habit of driving in knee socks, shorts, and wingtips) retired in 1957 after an admirable 19-win career, it was youngest brother Tim who would set the racing world reeling, winning 40 times in 189 attempts between 1949 and 1961 (still NASCAR's highest winning percentage),

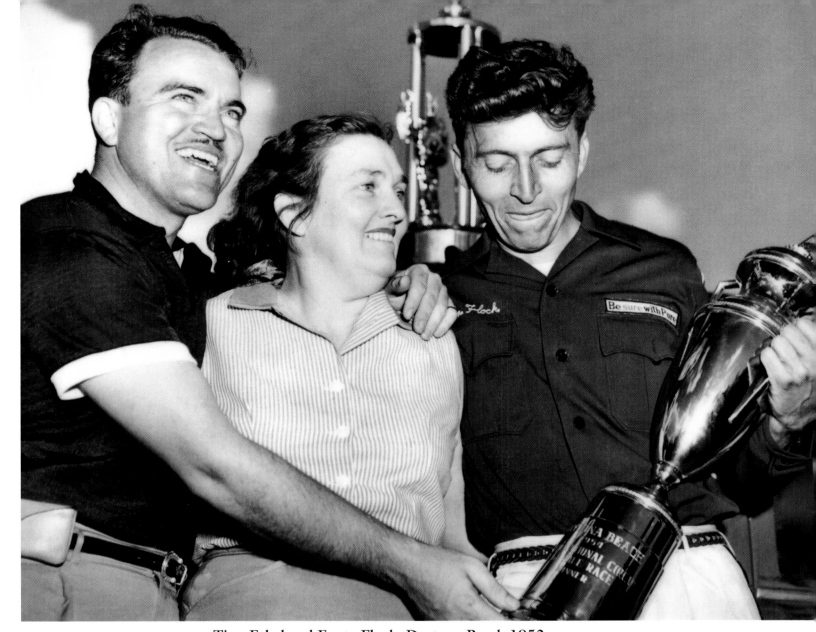

Tim, Ethel and Fonty Flock, Daytona Beach 1952.

capturing two Grand National (Cup Series) titles, and running eight laughable races with his vine-swinging compatriot Jocko as copilot.

NASCAR honcho Bill France could look past Flock's monkey business, but the two rough-hewn men locked horns over nearly everything else. When Flock, ignoring a Big Bill ultimatum, raced for extra cash at an "outlaw" track, France stripped him of hundreds of points, a move Flock claimed cost him the 1950 championship. And in 1954, Flock sat out most of the year in protest after France disallowed his early-season Daytona victory for alleged cheating.

The final straw came in 1961 when France banned Flock and Curtis Turner for life for attempting to unionize NASCAR drivers with the backing of the Teamsters. Flock was reinstated five years later, but with his salad days behind him, the forty-year-old legend decided to stay put. He never raced again.

In 1998 Tim Flock was honored as one of NASCAR's 50 Greatest Drivers. And along with Bob, Fonty, and Ethel, he still holds the curious distinction of being one of a record-setting four siblings to compete against each other in a top-level NASCAR race.

Richard Childress: NASCAR's Most Intimidating Team Owner
• • • • • • • • • •

In 1981 NASCAR driver Richard Childress took the biggest gamble of his life. After twelve winless seasons on the Cup circuit, the thirty-five-year-old also-ran decided to pack it in and hire someone else to race for him.

"It was the toughest thing I ever had to do," Childress said of that roll of the dice, which put 1980 Cup champion Dale Earnhardt behind the wheel. "I'd say it worked out, wouldn't you?"

In less than 14 years, Childress and Earnhardt became the most successful owner-driver partnership in the history of NASCAR, capturing a record six Cup championships between 1986 and 1994.

In less than fourteen years, Childress and Earnhardt would become the most successful owner-driver partnership in the history of NASCAR, capturing a record six Cup championships between 1986 and 1994. By 2000, they had run up sixty-seven victories and earned more than $40 millon, and their tear-your-head-off, Pittsburgh Steelers–style approach to winning had made Richard Childress Racing one of the most intimidating operations in all of NASCAR.

Like Junior Johnson before him, Childress took a hands-on, dirty-fingernail approach to ownership. As a driver, he'd built his own cars from scratch. As top dog he was just as likely to be found soaking up grease under the hood of the number 3 Chevy as behind a

desk haggling with sponsors. His skill at both tasks and his dedication inspired the rest of the team.

"I admire Richard because he started with nothing and built this thing to where it is today," said RCR crew chief Kevin Hamlin. "He understands this deal from the bottom up because he's a racer. He's not just some businessman who doesn't understand why everything doesn't go right all the time."

And sometimes things could go disastrously wrong. On February 18, 2001, the forty-nine-year-old Earnhardt, considered by many to be the greatest driver of all time, slammed head-on into the wall on

the last lap of the Daytona 500. He died instantly.

The devastated Childress thought about calling it quits. But he recalled, "Dale and I had a pact between us. Whatever happened, we needed to keep on racing." So like all great competitors, he climbed back on the horse.

Just three weeks later, Childress and his twenty-five-year-old rookie driver Kevin Harvick, who would go on to win Rookie of the Year honors, won the Cracker Barrel 500 in Atlanta, racing Earnhardt's repainted and renumbered Chevy—with a little help from Dale.

"When we got the lead, I just looked up in the sky and said, 'We need your help, buddy,' " Childress said after the tough race. "And he was there."

But living up to Earnhardt's legacy is a tough gambit. Although Childress has since gone on to notch two championships in NASCAR's Busch Series, making RCR the first operation to win titles at three levels (NASCAR Cup, Busch, and Craftsman Truck, in 1995), the tenacious three-car owner is still searching for the combination that will bring home his next Cup.

"I just want drivers that want it as bad as I want it," he said in 2004. "I want drivers with that fire and desire."

Car owner Richard Childress, center, and Dale Earnhardt wave to the crowd after winning the championship at Atlanta Raceway.

Jack Roush:
NASCAR Team Titan

• • • • • • • • •

Owner Jack Roush has been called many things during his eighteen-year tenure in NASCAR—the Mad Scientist, the Cat in the Hat, Mr. Conspiracy, and a few epithets that would singe the ears of a sailor—but until 2003, "champion" wasn't one of them.

The former Ford employee and motor sports junkie had arrived in NASCAR cocksure, a proven winner, having picked off dragster and

> *Owner Jack Roush has been called many things during his 18-year tenure in NASCAR—the Mad Scientist, the Cat in the Hat, Mr. Conspiracy, and a few epithets that would singe the ears of a sailor—but until 2003, "champion" wasn't one of them.*

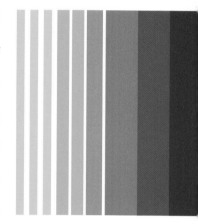

road-racing titles like fish in a barrel over the previous two decades. But adding a Cup crown to his overflowing trophy case would prove more difficult than just raising the rifle and taking aim.

After debuting with driver Mark Martin in 1988, Roush endured fifteen long winters of discontent, made worse by what he alleged was the dirty dealing of the NASCAR brass. "I honestly never thought NASCAR was going to allow me to win, no matter what I did," he once complained.

What he did was build one of the most formidable race teams in the sport, totaling five cars—the most in NASCAR—by 1998. He carved some nifty numbers along the way, including 66 wins and 368 top fives

Mark Martin, driver of the #6 Roush Racing Ford Taurus, speaks with car owner Jack Roush during qualifing for the Carolina Dodge Dealers 400 at Darlington Raceway in Darlington, South Carolina.

heading into the final stretch of 2003. But the stats didn't tell the whole story.

There were the four second-place points finishes and six third-place season bests, including Martin's slim 26-point loss to Dale Earnhardt in 1990 after being penalized 46 points for a rules infraction, and a similar loss to Tony Stewart (by 38 points) in 2002 after NASCAR again stripped points from Martin, just before the season finale.

For some, Roush's grousing about dirty tricks was nothing more than sour grapes from a man who'd poured too much time and too many millions into his operation to come away empty-handed. Others thought perhaps NASCAR *was* playing favorites, artificially leveling the field. After all, Roush never really fit the mold. With his floppy straw hat and wire-rimmed glasses, he looked more the type to be pruning daffodils and listening to public radio on Sundays than managing the rumblings of five 800-horsepower, 3,500-pound mechanical monsters.

But by November 9, 2003, none of that mattered, as Matt Kenseth's fourth-place finish at Rockingham locked up the first NASCAR Cup title for Roush Racing.

"I'm kind of in shock over the whole deal," he told reporters. "You have to understand, I have been so close before, close enough to touch it, and ended up so disappointed."

What he couldn't touch before he now sank his talons into. In 2004, three of his five drivers qualified for the Nextel Cup Chase; Kurt Busch brought home the crown. By the end of 2005, all five of Roush's cars were in the Chase.

"I don't think there was ever a question of whether it would happen for him," said Martin, still with the team in 2005. "It was just a matter of when."

Junior Johnson: Notorious Bootlegger to NASCAR Icon

• • • • • • • • •

From the time he could peer over the dashboard, Robert "Junior" Johnson was hell on wheels, hauling his family's black-market whiskey at warp speed through North Carolina's backwoods and hollows. This good ol' boy *knew* cars. Knew how to soup them up, knew how to fix them, knew how to make them do things nobody had ever seen before. After all, his freedom was at stake.

"Moonshiners put more time, energy, thought, and love into their cars than any racers ever will," Johnson once said. "Lose on the track and you go home. Lose with a load of whiskey and you go to jail."

While that classic bootlegger's knowledge of things mechanical would eventually make Johnson one of NASCAR's most successful and respected team owners, it was the fear of being nabbed that molded him into one of the hardest, fastest, scariest road

Junior Johnson peers from his car after winning the pole position for the Dixie 400 stock car race at the Atlanta International Raceway, June 3, 1964.

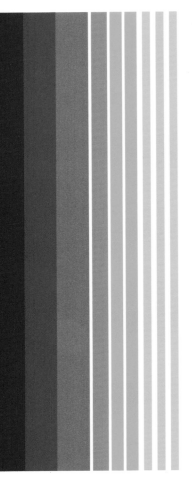

But Johnson's greatest legacy isn't to be found in his enviable stats, his racing talent, his business acumen, his team generalship, or even his legendary mechanical innovations. Rather, it lies in the savvy racing wisdom he has passed along to the army of drivers, builders, mechanics, crew chiefs, and others who have passed through his garage over the years—and all of NASCAR has been richer for it.

Over the next thirty years as an owner, Johnson would assemble some of the finest teams in racing, fielding a veritable who's who of top drivers, and would land some of NASCAR's richest sponsorship deals. Twenty-five times his racers finished tenth or better in points, and from 1976 to 1985 his drivers Cale Yarborough and Darrell Waltrip dominated the series, winning six Cup championships (a feat Johnson never once accomplished as a driver), delivering 79 of his 139 total victories, and earning nearly $7.5 million of his teams' $23.6 million overall take.

But Johnson's greatest legacy isn't to be found in his enviable stats, his racing talent, his business acumen, his team generalship, or even his legendary mechanical innovations. Rather, it lies in the savvy racing wisdom he has passed along to the army of drivers, builders, mechanics, crew chiefs, and others who have passed through his garage over the years—and all of NASCAR has been richer for it.

"That's what we called the University of Ronda [Johnson's hometown]," Darrell Waltrip said of Johnson's tutelage. "When you left there you had one of the best educations in racing that you could ever hope to get."

Johnson retired from racing in 1995. In 1998, he was honored as one of NASCAR's 50 Greatest Drivers.

warriors in the history of racing.

Between 1953 and 1965, minus a year in the federal penitentiary for tending the family's white lightning still, Junior Johnson was pure thunder on the track, racking up 50 wins (tenth all time) and 121 top five finishes in 313 races. He never stroked, never laid back, never paced like the others. It was full-throttle at all times, come hell or high water, wreck or win. "If that car didn't break or crash," remembered driver Tim Flock, "you could not catch him."

And then, after posting a career-high thirteen victories in 1965, the thirty-four-year-old Johnson abruptly called it quits and jumped into a new suit. "I think I enjoyed working on the cars more than I did driving them," he recalled. "I decided to turn the driving over to someone else."